HRW

ALGEBRA ONE
INTERACTIONS
COURSE 2

ASSESSMENT SOFTWARE ITEM LISTING

$$f(\ell) = \frac{6600}{\ell}$$

HOLT, RINEHART AND WINSTON
Harcourt Brace & Company

Austin · New York · Orlando · Atlanta · San Francisco · Boston · Dallas · Toronto · London

ISBN 0-03-051303-0

3 4 5 6 179 02 01 00

HRW
& ASSESSMENT SOFTWARE ITEM LISTING

SO CONVENIENT TOGETHER, YOU CAN...

FLIP THE PAGE TO:

- Quickly preview the quantity, quality, and variety of **every** question, answer, and illustration in the *Assessment Software* package

- Assemble a list of questions you intend to use before accessing the *Assessment Software*

- Pick from a variety of questions, including quantitative comparison, multiple choice, and short answer

- Select questions by objective, chapter, or specific lesson

CLICK THE MOUSE TO:

- Create worksheets, quizzes, mid-terms, and final exams

- Produce make-up exams or alternate tests using our handy revision function

- Scramble question order

- Review your tests, including graphics

- Select questions by number, preview, random selection— or write them yourself

TABLE OF CONTENTS

About the *HRW Algebra One Interactions Course 2 Item Listing* and *Assessment Software*

This *Item Listing* contains a complete printout of the test questions and answers from the *HRW Algebra One Interactions Course 2 Assessment Software*. With the *Item Listing*, you can quickly preview the variety of test items stored in the *Assessment Software* in order to assemble a list of questions that you intend to use for worksheets, quizzes, and tests.

The *User's Guide* that is included in the *Assessment Software* package contains directions for installing and using the program. Several options exist in the *Assessment Software* for selecting questions. You may choose questions with the random pick feature or select questions based on specific criteria.

Chapter Files

The questions are arranged by chapter and stored in 10 separate chapter files, one for each chapter in the textbook. Combinations of questions from any chapter may be used to generate a test.

Question Attributes

Each question is classified by attributes such as specific type, specific lesson, and lesson objective. The *Assessment Software* lets you select questions based on these attributes. See the *User's Guide* for instructions.

Question Types

Each chapter contains three different types of questions: Quantitative Comparison (Q), Multiple Choice (M), and Short Answer (S). When the program displays information about a question, it uses one of the one-letter abbreviations indicated.

Lesson Number

Each test question is coded with a section number that links the question to its respective lesson in the chapter.

Objective-Based Option

Each test question has an objective code that links the question to a lesson objective. Every lesson has two or three objectives, which are listed on the first page of the lesson in the *Teacher's Planning Guide*. See pages vi–ix for a complete listing of objectives.

How to Get Started

To get started, install the program on your computer's hard disk. The *User's Guide* describes how to perform this procedure in the Installation section.

Technical Support

The *User's Guide* should answer any questions you have about the program. However, if you need assistance, call the Holt, Rinehart and Winston Technical Support Center at 1-800-323-9239. You can also access a knowledge base of solutions to common problems and answers to common questions by calling the Technical Support Center's Fax on Demand Service at 1-800-352-1680.

In addition, you can contact the Technical Support Center through the World Wide Web at http://www.hrwtechsupport.com or by e-mail at tsc@hrwtechsupport.com.

LESSON OBJECTIVES

CHAPTER 1 Functions, Equations, and Inequalities

1a   Use the Addition and Subtraction Properties of Equality to solve equations.
2a   Use the Multiplication and Division Properties of Equality to solve equations.
3a   Use properties of equality to solve two-step equations.
4a   Use properties of equality and the Distributive Property to solve multistep equations.
5a   Use properties of inequality to solve inequalities.
5b   Graph solutions of inequalities on a number line.
6a   Use the definition of absolute value to solve equations and inequalities involving absolute value.

CHAPTER 2 Linear Functions and Systems

1a   Determine the slope of a line through two points by using a graph.
1b   Determine the slope of a line through two points by using the slope formula.
2a   Graph the equation of a line.
3a   Create tables, and graph systems of equations.
3b   Find an approximate solution to a system by inspecting a graph.
4a   Graph a system of equations, and estimate a solution from a graph by inspection.
4b   Find an exact solution to a system of equations by substituton.
5a   Find an exact solution to a system of equations by using the elimination method.
6a   Identify consistent and inconsistent systems of equations.
6b   Compare slopes and intercepts of independent and dependent systems.
7a   Determine the boundary line of the solution to a linear inequality.
7b   Graph the solution to a linear inequality.
7c   Graph the solution to a system of linear inequalities.
8a   Solve traditional application problems.

CHAPTER 3 Matrices

1a   Interpret data from given information, and write the data in table or matrix form.
1b   Determine the dimensions of a matrix, and locate an entry by its address.
1c   Determine whether two matrices are equal.
2a   Add and subtract matrices.
2b   Determine whether there is an additive identity for matrices.
3a   Multiply a matrix by a scalar, and multiply matrices.
3b   Determine the identity matrix for multiplication.
4a   Determine the inverse matrix for multiplication.
4b   Use technology to find the inverse of a matrix.
5a   Solve a system of equations by using matrices.
5b   Use technology to solve a system of equations by using matrices.

CHAPTER 4 Probability and Statistics

1a   Find the experimental probability that an event will occur.
1b   Use random numbers in probability situations.

2a   Design and perform simulations to find experimental probability.

3a   Find the mean, median, and mode of a set of data.
3b   Make scatter plots and frequency tables from data.

4a   Draw and interpret Venn diagrams.
4b   Apply the Addition Principle of Counting.

5a   Make a tree diagram to show possible outcomes.
5b   Use the Multiplication Principle of Counting to find the number of possible outcomes.

6a   Find the theoretical probability that an event will occur.
6b   Use counting principles to find the probability that an event will occur.

7a   Define and give examples of independent events.
7b   Find the probability that independent events will occur.

CHAPTER 5 Transformations

1a   Understand the definitions of relation and function.
1b   Use a graph to identify a function with the vertical-line test.
1c   Use the function notation, $f(x)$, to represent and evaluate a function.

2a   Identify basic transformations of parent functions.
2b   Define *stretch*, *reflect*, and *shift* as they apply to the graphs of functions.

3a   Describe the effect of a stretch on the graph of a function when the coefficient is greater than or equal to 1 and when it is between 0 and 1.
3b   Identify the coefficient to determine the amount of stretch.

4a   Understand the connection between the reflection of a graph and the opposite of a function.
4b   Identify the minimum or maximum value for absolute-value and quadratic functions.

5a   Describe the effect of a translation on the graph of a function.
5b   Identify the relationship between the translation of a graph and the addition or subtraction of a constant to the function.

6a   Identify the parent function for a transformation.
6b   Understand the effect of order on combining transformations.

CHAPTER 6 Exponents

1a   Understand the concepts of exponents and powers.
1b   Use the properties of exponents to simplify expressions.

2a   Understand the structure and concept of a monomial.
2b   Use the properties of exponents to simplify expressions.

3a   Understand the concept of negative and zero exponents.
3b   Simplify expressions containing negative and zero exponents.

CHAPTER 1: *Functions, Equations, and Inequalities*

QUANTITATIVE COMPARISON

In the space provided, write:
a. if the quantity in Column A is greater than the quantity in Column B;
b. if the quantity in Column B is greater than the quantity in Column A;
c. if the two quantities are equal; or
d. if the relationship cannot be determined from the information given.

Column A	Column B	Answer

1.

The solution to $x + 12 = 15$	The solution to $x - 2 = 5$	_____

2.

The solution to $12x = 60$	The solution to $-8x = -40$	_____

3.

The solution to $5x + 2 = 32$	The solution to $6x + 3 = 45$	_____

4.

The solution to $3x + 4 = 2x + 6$	The solution to $6x + 9 = 7x + 8$	_____

5.

The smallest solution to $2x + 3 > 11$	The largest solution to $-2x + 3 > 15$	_____

6.

$|x - 5|$	$|x - 8|$	_____

MULTIPLE CHOICE. Circle the letter of the best answer choice.

7. Solve for x: $x + 9 = 5$.
   a. $x = 14$ b. $x = -14$ c. $x = 4$ d. $x = -4$

8. Solve for x: $4 = x + 12$.
   a. $x = 8$ b. $x = -8$ c. $x = 16$ d. $x = -16$

9. Solve for x: $x + 15 = -10$.
   a. $x = -5$ b. $x = 5$ c. $x = -25$ d. $x = 25$

10. Solve for y: $y - 7 = 13$.
    a. $y = 20$ b. $y = -20$ c. $y = 6$ d. $y = -6$

11. Solve for y: $-18 = y - 6$.
    a. $y = 24$ b. $y = -24$ c. $y = 12$ d. $y = -12$

12. Solve for y: $y - 4 = -14$.
   a. $y = 10$ b. $y = -10$ c. $y = 18$ d. $y = -18$

13. The sale price of an item is \$24 less than the retail price of the item. If the sale price of the item is \$80, what is the retail price of the item?
   a. \$46   b. \$56   c. \$94   d. \$104

14. Solve for x: $-63 = 7x$.
   a. $x = -441$ b. $x = -70$ c. $x = -56$ d. $x = -9$

15. Solve for x: $\frac{4}{5}x = 20$.
   a. $x = -25$ b. $x = 25$ c. $x = -16$ d. $x = 16$

16. Solve for x: $\frac{x}{5} = -9$.
   a. $x = -45$ b. $x = -14$ c. $x = -4$ d. $x = -1.4$

17. Solve for x: $12 = \frac{x}{-7}$.
   a. $x = -5$ b. $x = 19$ c. $x = -84$ d. $x = 5$

18. Solve the proportion: $\frac{x}{-5} = \frac{-12}{20}$.
   a. $x = 80$ b. $x = 40$ c. $x = 5$ d. $x = 3$

19. Solve the proportion: $\frac{6}{7} = \frac{-78}{x}$.
   a. $x = -552$ b. $x = -91$ c. $x = -164$ d. $x = -42$

20. A state charges 6% sales tax on the price of any item bought in the state. If the sales tax on an item is \$9, what is the price of the item?
   a. \$0.54   b. \$9.06   c. \$150   d. \$250

21. Solve for x: $8x - 16 = 40$.
   a. $x = 3$ b. $x = 7$ c. $x = 24$ d. $x = 48$

22. Solve for x: $15 + 5x = 65$.
   a. $x = 45$ b. $x = 16$ c. $x = 10$ d. $x = 4$

23. Solve for x: $-8 = 4x - 32$.
   a. $x = -8$ b. $x = 20$ c. $x = -10$ d. $x = 6$

24. Solve for x: $\frac{x}{-6} + 18 = 24$.
   a. $x = -252$ b. $x = -36$ c. $x = -1$ d. $x = 0$

25. Solve for x: $14 = 21 + \frac{x}{7}$.
   a. $x = -49$ b. $x = 49$ c. $x = -1$ d. $x = 1$

26. Solve for x: $\frac{2}{5}x + 12 = 32$.
   a. $x = 8$ b. $x = -8$ c. $x = 50$ d. $x = -50$

27. Solve for x: $\frac{-3}{7}x - 6 = 15$.
   a. $x = -9$ b. $x = -15$ c. $x = -21$ d. $x = -49$

28. Solve for x: $7x + 12 = 3x + 36$.
    a. $x = -6$ b. $x = 6$ c. $x = -12$ d. $x = 12$

29. Solve for x: $30 + 4x = 9x - 15$.
    a. $x = -3$ b. $x = 3$ c. $x = -9$ d. $x = 9$

30. Solve for x: $-4x + 20 = 50 + 6x$.
    a. $x = -3$ b. $x = 3$ c. $x = -35$ d. $x = 35$

31. Solve for x: $-6x - 65 = -5x + 25 + 9x$.
    a. $x = 45$ b. $x = -45$ c. $x = 9$ d. $x = -9$

32. Solve for x: $3x + 4(x - 2) = 9x + 7 - 5x$.
    a. $x = 8$ b. $x = -8$ c. $x = 5$ d. $x = -5$

33. Solve for x: $6x - 3(x + 2) = 10x + 22 - 3x$.
    a. $x = 7$ b. $x = -7$ c. $x = 3.5$ d. $x = -3.5$

34. Claire wants to rent a car. Company A charges $50 plus $10 a day. Company B charges $20 plus $15 a day. After how many days will the two costs be the same?
    a. 3 days   b. 6 days   c. 10 days   d. 15 days

35. Solve for x: $2x - 10 > 16$.
    a. $x < 3$ b. $x < 13$ c. $x > 3$ d. $x > 13$

36. Solve for x: $6 \leq 4x + 30$.
    a. $-4 \leq x$ b. $-6 \leq x$ c. $4 \leq x$ d. $6 \leq x$

37. Solve for x: $\frac{x}{5} - 6 > -10$.
    a. $x < -80$ b. $x < -20$ c. $x > -80$ d. $x > -20$

38. Solve for x: $\frac{x}{-4} + 8 \geq 12$.
    a. $x \leq -16$ b. $x \leq -80$ c. $x \geq -16$ d. $x \geq -80$

39. Solve for x: $25 > -5x - 10$.
    a. $7 > x$ b. $3 > x$ c. $-7 < x$ d. $-3 < x$

40. Solve for x: $\frac{4}{5}x - 12 \leq 28$.
    a. $x \leq 20$ b. $x \leq 50$ c. $x \geq 20$ d. $x \geq 50$

41. Solve for x: $\frac{-3}{8}x + 20 < 38$.
    a. $x < 48$ b. $x < -48$ c. $x > 48$ d. $x > -48$

42. Solve for x: $|x + 5| = 8$.
    a. $x = 3$ or $x = -3$ b. $x = -3$ or $x = 13$
    c. $x = 3$ or $x = 13$ d. $x = 3$ or $x = -13$

43. Solve for x: $|3x + 9| = 15$.
    a. $x = 2$ or $x = -2$ b. $x = 2$ or $x = -8$
    c. $x = -2$ or $x = 8$ d. $x = -2$ or $x = -8$

44. Solve for x: $|4x - 12| = 40$.
    a. $x = 13$ or $x = -13$ b. $x = 7$ or $x = -13$
    c. $x = -7$ or $x = 13$ d. $x = -7$ or $x = -13$

45. Solve for x: $|2x + 6| \leq 14$.
   a. $-10 \leq x \leq 4$
   b. $10 \geq x \geq -4$
   c. $-10 \geq x \geq 4$
   d. $10 \leq x \leq -4$

46. Solve for x: $|5x - 20| < 10$.
   a. $-6 < x < -2$
   b. $2 < x < 6$
   c. $-6 > x > -2$
   d. $2 > x > 6$

47. Solve for x: $|6x + 24| \geq 18$.
   a. $x \geq -7$ or $x \leq -1$
   b. $x \geq 7$ or $x \leq 1$
   c. $x \geq -1$ or $x \leq -7$
   d. $x \geq 1$ or $x \leq 7$

48. Solve for x: $|7x - 21| > 35$.
   a. $x > -8$ or $x < 2$
   b. $x > -2$ or $x < 8$
   c. $x < -2$ or $x < 8$
   d. $x < -2$ or $x > 8$

SHORT ANSWER. Write the answer in the space provided.

49. Solve for x: $x + 17 = 30$.

   _____

50. Solve for x: $14 = x + 20$.

   _____

51. Solve for x: $x + 9 = -12$.

   _____

52. Solve for y: $y - 16 = 5$.

   _____

53. Solve for y: $y - 24 = -10$.

   _____

54. Solve for y: $y - 15 = -22$.

   _____

55. There are 32 fewer seniors at Central High School this year than last year. Using x as the number of seniors last year, write an equation to show that the number of seniors this year is 540. Solve the equation to find the number of seniors last year.

   _____

56. Solve for x: $-9.6 = -2.4x$.

   _____

57. Solve for x: $\frac{5}{8}x = -30$.

   _____

4

58. Solve for x: $\dfrac{x}{9} = 27$.

_____

59. Solve for x: $\dfrac{x}{-4} = -20$.

_____

60. Solve the proportion: $\dfrac{11}{-6} = \dfrac{x}{54}$.

_____

61. Solve the proportion: $\dfrac{9}{x} = \dfrac{135}{-120}$.

_____

62. The property taxes in a town are 7% of the assessed value of the property. The property tax on a piece of property in the town is \$1750. Using x as the value of the property, write and solve an equation to find the value of the property.

_____

63. Solve for x: $12x - 15 = 81$.

_____

64. Solve for x: $117 = 12 + 15x$.

_____

65. Solve for x: $\dfrac{x}{14} + 15 = 10$.

_____

66. Solve for x: $-20 = \dfrac{x}{-9} - 8$.

_____

67. Solve for x: $\dfrac{5}{9}x + 23 = 8$.

_____

68. Solve for x: $25 = \dfrac{-3}{8}x - 17$.

_____

69. Sarah wants to invest \$4000 at 9% and the rest at 5%. How much should she invest at 5% if she wants to earn a total of \$500 in interest? Write and solve an equation using x as the amount invested at 5%.

_____

5

70. Solve for x: $9x - 14 = 3x + 34$.

   _____

71. Solve for x: $11 + 8x = 15x + 60$.

   _____

72. Solve for x: $55 + 5x = -7x - 5$.

   _____

73. Solve for x: $7x + 82 - 3x = 14 + 8x$.

   _____

74. Solve for x: $5x + 2(x + 4) = 10x - 22$.

   _____

75. Solve for x: $16x - 195 = 7x - 3(x + 5)$.

   _____

76. Kurt wants to rent a moving van. Company A charges $30 plus $24 a day. Company B charges $72 plus $18 a day. After how many days will the charges be the same? Using x as the number of days, write and solve an equation to represent the problem.

   _____

77. Solve for x: $\dfrac{x}{-6} - 5 > 4$.

   _____

78. Solve for x: $\dfrac{5}{9}x + 12 \le 37$.

   _____

79. Solve for x: $\dfrac{-6}{7}x - 15 < 21$.

   _____

80. Solve for x. Graph your solution on a number line.
   $15 + 9x > 42$

   _____

81. Solve for x. Graph your solution on a number line.
   $18 \ge -5x - 17$

   _____

82. Solve for x. Graph your solution on a number line.
   $12 + \dfrac{x}{8} < 10$

   _____

83. Solve for x. Graph your solution on a number line.

$\dfrac{x}{-3} - 5 \geq -3$

———————————

84. Solve for x: $|4x + 24| = 32$.

———————————

85. Solve for x: $|10x - 35| = 65$.

———————————

86. Solve for x. Graph your solution on a number line.

$|3x - 15| < 6$

———————————

87. Solve for x. Graph your solution on a number line.

$|7x + 42| \leq 35$

———————————

88. Solve for x. Graph your solution on a number line.

$|5x + 30| > 40$

———————————

89. Solve for x. Graph your solution on a number line.

$|8x - 32| \geq 16$

———————————

90. A gear must be 24 mm wide. The tolerance is ±0.3 mm. Using x as the width of the gears, write an absolute-value inequality to show the acceptable widths of the gears. Solve the inequality.

————————————————————————————

1. Answer: b Section: 1 Objective: 1a

2. Answer: c Section: 2 Objective: 2a

3. Answer: b Section: 3 Objective: 3a

4. Answer: a Section: 4 Objective: 4a

5. Answer: a Section: 5 Objective: 5a

6. Answer: d Section: 6 Objective: 6a

7. Answer: d. $x = -4$ Section: 1 Objective: 1a

8. Answer: b. $x = -8$ Section: 1 Objective: 1a

9. Answer: c. $x = -25$ Section: 1 Objective: 1a

10. Answer: a. $y = 20$ Section: 1 Objective: 1a

11. Answer: d. $y = -12$ Section: 1 Objective: 1a

12. Answer: b. $y = -10$ Section: 1 Objective: 1a

13. Answer: d. $104 Section: 1 Objective: 1a

14. Answer: d. $x = -9$ Section: 2 Objective: 2a

15. Answer: b. $x = 25$ Section: 2 Objective: 2a

16. Answer: a. $x = -45$ Section: 2 Objective: 2a

17. Answer: c. $x = -84$ Section: 2 Objective: 2a

18. Answer: d. $x = 3$ Section: 2 Objective: 2a

19. Answer: b. $x = -91$ Section: 2 Objective: 2a

20. Answer: c. $150 Section: 2 Objective: 2a

21. Answer: b. $x = 7$ Section: 3 Objective: 3a

22. Answer: c. $x = 10$ Section: 3 Objective: 3a

23. Answer: d. $x = 6$ Section: 3 Objective: 3a

24. Answer: b. $x = -36$ Section: 3 Objective: 3a

25. Answer: a. $x = -49$ Section: 3 Objective: 3a

26. Answer: c. $x = 50$ Section: 3   Objective: 3a

27. Answer: d. $x = -49$ Section: 3   Objective: 3a

28. Answer: b. $x = 6$ Section: 4   Objective: 4a

29. Answer: d. $x = 9$ Section: 4   Objective: 4a

30. Answer: a. $x = -3$ Section: 4   Objective: 4a

31. Answer: d. $x = -9$ Section: 4   Objective: 4a

32. Answer: c. $x = 5$ Section: 4   Objective: 4a

33. Answer: b. $x = -7$ Section: 4   Objective: 4a

34. Answer: b. 6 days   Section: 4   Objective: 4a

35. Answer: d. $x > 13$ Section: 5   Objective: 5a

36. Answer: b. $-6 \leq x$ Section: 5   Objective: 5a

37. Answer: d. $x > -20$ Section: 5   Objective: 5a

38. Answer: a. $x \leq -16$ Section: 5   Objective: 5a

39. Answer: c. $-7 < x$ Section: 5   Objective: 5a

40. Answer: b. $x \leq 50$ Section: 5   Objective: 5a

41. Answer: d. $x > -48$ Section: 5   Objective: 5a

42. Answer: d. $x = 3$ or $x = -13$ Section: 6   Objective: 6a

43. Answer: b. $x = 2$ or $x = -8$ Section: 6   Objective: 6a

44. Answer: c. $x = -7$ or $x = 13$ Section: 6   Objective: 6a

45. Answer: a. $-10 \leq x \leq 4$ Section: 6   Objective: 6a

46. Answer: b. $2 < x < 6$ Section: 6   Objective: 6a

47. Answer: c. $x \geq -1$ or $x \leq -7$ Section: 6   Objective: 6a

48. Answer: d. $x < -2$ or $x > 8$ Section: 6   Objective: 6a

49. Answer: $x = 13$ Section: 1   Objective: 1a

50. Answer: $x = -6$ Section: 1   Objective: 1a

51. Answer: $x = -21$ Section: 1   Objective: 1a

52. Answer: $y = 21$ Section: 1   Objective: 1a

53. Answer: $y = 14$ Section: 1   Objective: 1a

54. Answer: $y = -7$ Section: 1   Objective: 1a

55. Answer: $x - 32 = 540$; $x = 572$; there were 572 seniors last year. Section: 1

Objective: 1a

56. Answer: $x = 4$ Section: 2 Objective: 2a

57. Answer: $x = -48$ Section: 2 Objective: 2a

58. Answer: $x = 243$ Section: 2 Objective: 2a

59. Answer: $x = 80$ Section: 2 Objective: 2a

60. Answer: $x = -99$ Section: 2 Objective: 2a

61. Answer: $x = -8$ Section: 2 Objective: 2a

62. Answer: $0.07x = 1750$; $x = 25,000$; the value of the property is \$25,000. Section: 2

Objective: 2a

63. Answer: $x = 8$ Section: 3 Objective: 3a

64. Answer: $x = 7$ Section: 3 Objective: 3a

65. Answer: $x = -70$ Section: 3 Objective: 3a

66. Answer: $x = 108$ Section: 3 Objective: 3a

67. Answer: $x = -27$ Section: 3 Objective: 3a

68. Answer: $x = -112$ Section: 3 Objective: 3a

69. Answer: $360 + 0.05x = 500$; $x = 2800$; Sarah should invest \$2800 at 5%. Section: 3

Objective: 3a

70. Answer: $x = 8$ Section: 4 Objective: 4a

71. Answer: $x = -7$ Section: 4 Objective: 4a

72. Answer: $x = -5$ Section: 4 Objective: 4a

73. Answer: $x = 17$ Section: 4 Objective: 4a

74. Answer: $x = 10$ Section: 4 Objective: 4a

75. Answer: $x = 15$ Section: 4 Objective: 4a

76. Answer: $30 + 24x = 72 + 18x$; $x = 7$; the cost will be the same for 7 days. Section: 4

Objective: 4a

77. Answer: $x < -54$ Section: 5 Objective: 5a

78. Answer: $x \le 45$ Section: 5   Objective: 5a

79. Answer: $x > -42$ Section: 5   Objective: 5a

80. Answer: $x > 3$

Section: 5   Objective: 5b

81. Answer: $-7 \le x$

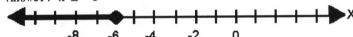

Section: 5   Objective: 5b

82. Answer: $x < -16$

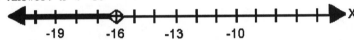

Section: 5   Objective: 5b

83. Answer: $x \le -6$

Section: 5   Objective: 5b

84. Answer: $x = 2$ or $x = -14$ Section: 6   Objective: 6a

85. Answer: $x = 10$ or $x = -3$ Section: 6   Objective: 6a

86. Answer: $3 < x < 7$

Section: 6   Objective: 6a

87. Answer: $-11 \le x \le -1$

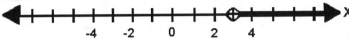

Section: 6   Objective: 6a

88. Answer: $x > 2$ or $x < -14$

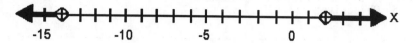

Section: 6 Objective: 6a

89. Answer: $x \geq 6$ or $x \leq 2$

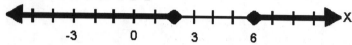

Section: 6 Objective: 6a

90. Answer: $|x - 24| \leq 0.3$; $23.7 \leq x \leq 24.3$ Section: 6 Objective: 6a

CHAPTER 2: Linear Functions and Systems

QUANTITATIVE COMPARISON

In the space provided, write:
a. if the quantity in Column A is greater than the quantity in Column B;
b. if the quantity in Column B is greater than the quantity in Column A;
c. if the two quantities are equal; or
d. if the relationship cannot be determined from the information given.

Column A	Column B	Answer

1.

| The slope of the line through the points (2, 5) and (4, 10) | The slope of the line through the points (4, 5) and (2, 10) | _____ |

2.

| The slope of the line with equation $y = 4x - 8$ | The slope of the line with equation $8x + 4y = 8$ | _____ |

3.

| The y-coordinate of the solution to the system of equations graphed | The x-coordinate of the solution to the system of equations graphed | _____ |

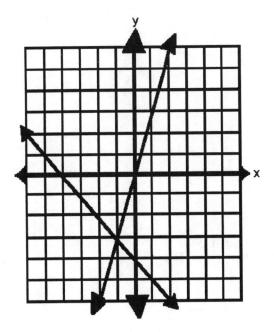

4.

The value of x in the solution to $\begin{cases} x - 3y = 5 \\ 2x + 4y = 0 \end{cases}$	The value of y in the solution to $\begin{cases} x - 3y = 5 \\ 2x + 4y = 0 \end{cases}$

_____

5.

The value of x in the solution to $\begin{cases} 2x + y = 1 \\ 3x - y = -11 \end{cases}$	The value of y in the solution to $\begin{cases} 2x + y = 1 \\ 3x - y = -11 \end{cases}$

_____

6.

The number of solutions to the system $\begin{cases} y = 3x + 4 \\ y = 3x + 6 \end{cases}$	The number of solutions to the system $\begin{cases} y = 2x + 4 \\ y = 3x + 6 \end{cases}$

_____

7.

The x-coordinates of the points in the solutions to the system of inequalities graphed	The y-coordinates of the points in the solutions to the system of inequalities graphed

_____

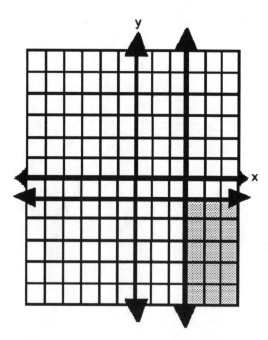

8. Gale buys 5 shirts and 2 pairs of shorts at a sale for $80.
At the same sale Sam buys 6 shirts and 1 pair of shorts for $82.

The price of shorts at the sale	The price of shirts at the sale

_____

MULTIPLE CHOICE. Circle the letter of the best answer choice.

9. Find the slope of the line graphed here.

    a. 4   b. -4   c. $\frac{1}{4}$ b. $\frac{-1}{4}$

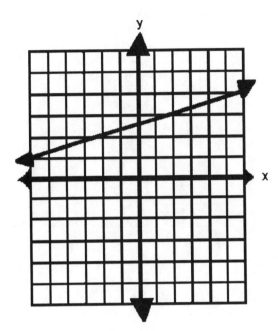

10. Find the slope of the line graphed here.

    a. -2   b. 2   c. $\frac{-1}{2}$ d. $\frac{1}{2}$

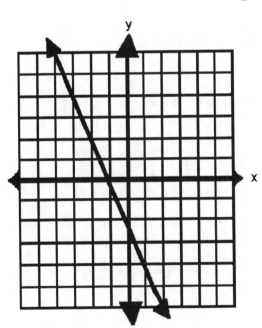

15

11. Find the slope of the line graphed here.
    a. 1   b. 0   c. -1   d. undefined

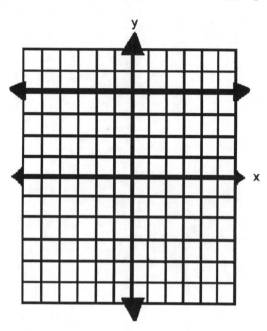

12. Find the slope of the line through the points (5, 8) and (7, 14).
    a. $\dfrac{1}{3}$ b. $\dfrac{-1}{3}$ c. 3   d. -3

13. Find the slope of the line through the points (6, -5) and (2, 11).
    a. -4   b. 4   c. $\dfrac{-1}{4}$ d. $\dfrac{1}{4}$

14. Find the slope of the line through the points (-1, 7) and (2, 9).
    a. $\dfrac{3}{2}$ b. $\dfrac{-3}{2}$ c. $\dfrac{2}{3}$ d. $\dfrac{-2}{3}$

15. Find the slope of the line through the points (10, 5) and (5, 8).
    a. $\dfrac{3}{5}$ b. $\dfrac{-3}{5}$ c. $\dfrac{5}{3}$ d. $\dfrac{-5}{3}$

16. Find the slope and y-intercept of the line with equation $y = -5 + 3x$.
    a. slope -5; y-intercept (0, 3)   b. slope 5; y-intercept (0, 3)
    c. slope 3; y-intercept (0, 5)   d. slope 3; y-intercept (0, -5)

17. Which of the following is an equation of the line with a slope of 4 and a y-intercept of 8?
    a. $y = 8x + 4$ b. $y = 4x + 8$ c. $y = -8 + 4x$ d. $y = 4 + 8x$

18. Find the x-intercept and y-intercept of the line with the equation $3x - 4y = 36$.
    a. (9, 0); (0, 12)   b. (12, 0); (0, 9)
    c. (-12, 0); (0, 9)   d. (12, 0); (0, -9)

19. Find the x-intercept and y-intercept of the line with the equation $-5x + 2y = 40$.
    a. (8, 0); (0, 20)   b. (-8, 0); (0, 20)
    c. (20, 0); (0, 8)   d. (20, 0); (0, -8)

20. Find the slope of the line with the equation $4x + 2y = 12$.
    a. -2   b. $\dfrac{-1}{2}$ c. $\dfrac{1}{3}$ d. 6

21. Find the slope of the line with the equation $-6x + 5y = 2$.

    a. $\dfrac{-6}{5}$ b. $\dfrac{6}{5}$ c. $\dfrac{-2}{5}$ d. $\dfrac{2}{5}$

22. Which of the following is an equation of the line through the points (2, 9) and (5, 15)?

    a. $y = \dfrac{1}{2}x + 8$ b. $y = \dfrac{-1}{2}x + 10$ c. $y = 2x + 5$ d. $y = -2x + 13$

23. Which of the following points is a solution to this system of equations: $\begin{cases} 3x + 2y = 5 \\ 5x + 3y = 9 \end{cases}$?

    a. (2, 3)   b. (3, 2)   c. (3, -2)   d. (-3, 2)

24. Which of the following points is a solution to this system of equations: $\begin{cases} -2x + 7y = 39 \\ 3x - 6y = -36 \end{cases}$?

    a. (2, 5)   b. (-2, 5)   c. (2, -5)   d. (5, -2)

25. Which of the following points is a solution to this system of equations: $\begin{cases} 5x - 9y = -6 \\ -3x - 6y = 15 \end{cases}$?

    a. (3, 1)   b. (-3, 1)   c. (3, -1)   d. (-3, -1)

26. Find the solution to the system of equations graphed.

    a. (-1, 3)   b. (3, -1)   c. (-1, -3)   d. (-3, -1)

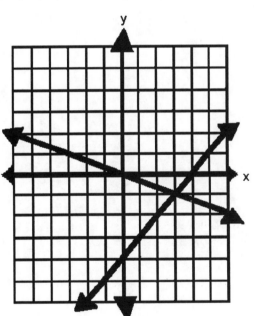

27. Find the solution to the system of equations graphed.
   a. (-1, 2)   b. (2, -1)   c. (-1, -2)   d. (-2, -1)

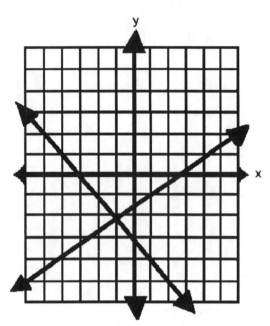

28. Find the solution to the system of equations graphed.
   a. (0, 3)   b. (3, 0)   c. (0, -3)   d. (-3, 0)

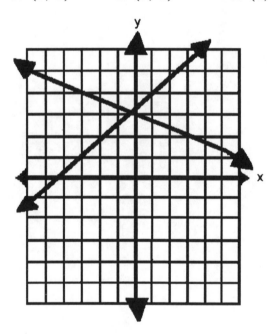

29. Find the solution to the system of equations graphed.
   a. (0, 4)   b. (0, -4)   c. (4, 0)   d. (-4, 0)

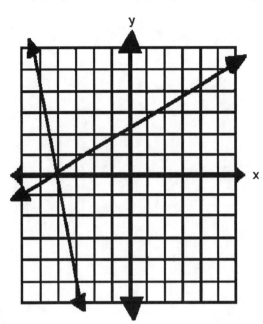

30. Solve by using the substitution method: $\begin{cases} 3x + y = 1 \\ 4x - y = 13 \end{cases}$.

   a. $x = 2$, $y = 5$ b. $x = -2$, $y = 5$ c. $x = 2$, $y = -5$ d. $x = -2$, $y = -5$

31. Solve by using the substitution method: $\begin{cases} -3x + y = 7 \\ -2x + 3y = -7 \end{cases}$.

   a. $x = -4$, $y = -5$ b. $x = 4$, $y = -5$ c. $x = -4$, $y = 5$ d. $x = 4$, $y = 5$

32. Solve by using the substitution method: $\begin{cases} 4x + 3y = -6 \\ x - 2y = 15 \end{cases}$.

   a. $x = -3$, $y = -6$ b. $x = 3$, $y = -6$ c. $x = -3$, $y = 6$ d. $x = 3$, $y = 6$

33. Solve by using the substitution method: $\begin{cases} x + 6y = -1 \\ -3x + 3y = 17 \end{cases}$.

   a. $x = 5$, $y = \dfrac{2}{3}$ b. $x = \dfrac{2}{3}$, $y = -5$ c. $x = \dfrac{-2}{3}$, $y = -5$ d. $x = -5$, $y = \dfrac{2}{3}$

34. Solve by using the substitution method: $\begin{cases} 4x = y - 9 \\ 2y = -8x + 6 \end{cases}$.

   a. $x = 6$, $y = \dfrac{-3}{4}$ b. $x = \dfrac{3}{4}$, $y = -6$ c. $x = -6$, $y = \dfrac{3}{4}$ d. $x = \dfrac{-3}{4}$, $y = 6$

35. Solve by using the substitution method: $\begin{cases} -3x = -6y + 9 \\ 4y = x + 2 \end{cases}$.

   a. $x = 4$, $y = \dfrac{-1}{2}$ b. $x = \dfrac{1}{2}$, $y = -4$ c. $x = -4$, $y = \dfrac{-1}{2}$ d. $x = \dfrac{1}{2}$, $y = 4$

36. Solve by using the substitution method: $\begin{cases} -4x = 3y - 26 \\ -2y - x = -14 \end{cases}$.

   a. $x = -6$, $y = \dfrac{2}{3}$ b. $x = -6$, $y = \dfrac{-2}{3}$ c. $x = 2$, $y = -6$ d. $x = 2$, $y = 6$

37. Solve by using the elimination method: $\begin{cases} -3x + 2y = -23 \\ 3x - 4y = 31 \end{cases}$.

   a. $x = 8$, $y = 4$ b. $x = 5$, $y = -19$ c. $x = 5$, $y = -4$ d. $x = -3$, $y = -10$

38. Solve by using the elimination method: $\begin{cases} 4x - 2y = -26 \\ -3x - 2y = -5 \end{cases}$
   a. $x = 4,\ y = 26$ b. $x = -3,\ y = 7$
   c. $x = 3,\ y = -14$ d. $x = -7,\ y = -13$

39. Solve by using the elimination method: $\begin{cases} -5x + 3y = 11 \\ 2x - y = -5 \end{cases}$
   a. $x = 2,\ y = 7$ b. $x = 4,\ y = 10$ c. $x = 5,\ y = 15$ d. $x = -4,\ y = -3$

40. Solve by using the elimination method: $\begin{cases} 4x + 6y = 4 \\ 2x - 9y = -2 \end{cases}$
   a. $x = \dfrac{1}{2},\ y = \dfrac{-2}{3}$ b. $x = \dfrac{1}{3},\ y = \dfrac{3}{4}$ c. $x = \dfrac{1}{2},\ y = \dfrac{1}{3}$ d. $x = \dfrac{1}{4},\ y = \dfrac{1}{2}$

41. Solve by using the elimination method: $\begin{cases} 3x - 4y = -9 \\ -4x + 12y = 17 \end{cases}$
   a. $x = \dfrac{1}{3},\ y = \dfrac{5}{2}$ b. $x = -2,\ y = \dfrac{3}{4}$ c. $x = \dfrac{1}{2},\ y = \dfrac{-2}{3}$ d. $x = 5,\ y = 6$

42. Solve by using the elimination method: $\begin{cases} 2x + 4y = 6 \\ 3x + 3y = -9 \end{cases}$
   a. $x = -9,\ y = 6$ b. $x = 12,\ y = -4$ c. $x = 9,\ y = -3$ d. $x = -5,\ y = 4$

43. Solve by using the elimination method: $\begin{cases} 6x - 8y = -4 \\ -9x + 12y = 6 \end{cases}$
   a. $x = \dfrac{3}{4},\ y = \dfrac{5}{2}$ b. $x = \dfrac{-2}{3},\ y = \dfrac{-1}{2}$ c. $x = \dfrac{1}{3},\ y = \dfrac{3}{4}$ d. $x = \dfrac{-2}{3},\ y = \dfrac{1}{3}$

44. What kind of system is graphed here?
   a. independent   b. dependent   c. inconsistent   d. none of these

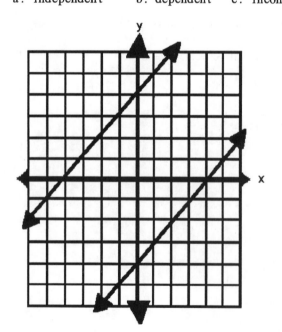

45. What kind of system is graphed here?
    a. independent   b. dependent   c. inconsistent   d. none of these

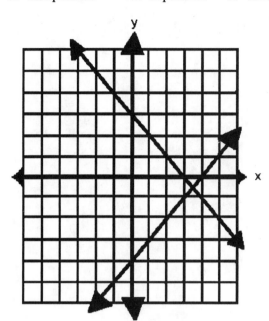

46. What kind of system is this: $\begin{cases} y = 3x + 8 \\ y = 5x + 8 \end{cases}$?
    a. independent   b. dependent   c. inconsistent   d. none of these

47. What kind of system is this: $\begin{cases} -2x + y = 5 \\ -4x + 2y = 10 \end{cases}$?
    a. independent   b. dependent   c. inconsistent   d. none of these

48. Which of the following is true in an inconsistent system of equations?
    a. The slopes and the y-intercepts of the lines are the same.
    b. The slopes of the lines are the same, and the y-intercepts of the lines are different.
    c. The slopes of the lines are different, and the y-intercepts of the lines are the same.
    d. The slopes and the y-intercepts of the lines are different.

49. Which of the following is true in a dependent system of equations?
    a. The slopes and the y-intercepts of the lines are the same.
    b. The slopes of the lines are the same, and the y-intercepts of the lines are different.
    c. The slopes of the lines are different, and the y-intercepts of the lines are the same.
    d. The slopes and the y-intercepts of the lines are different.

50. Which of the following equations would form an independent system of equations when combined with $y = 3x + 1$?
    a. $y = 3x - 1$ b. $3y = 9x + 3$ c. $y = -3x + 1$ d. $y = 3x + 8$

51. Which of the following is the boundary line for the graph of $3x + 4y \leq 12$?
    a. $3x + 4y < 12$ b. $3x + 4y > 12$ c. $3x + 4y = 12$ d. $3x + 4y \leq 12$

52. Which inequality is graphed here?
   a. $y \geq x - 2$ b. $y > x - 2$ c. $y \leq x - 2$ d. $y < x - 2$

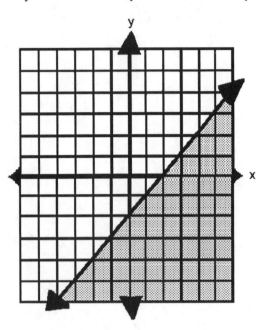

53. Which inequality is graphed here?
   a. $y > -2x + 4$ b. $y \geq -2x + 4$ c. $y < -2x + 4$ d. $y \leq -2x + 4$

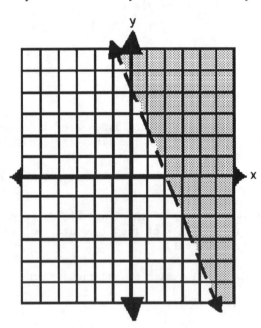

54. Which system of inequalities is graphed here?

a. $\begin{cases} x < -3 \\ y > -2 \end{cases}$ b. $\begin{cases} x \leq -3 \\ y > -2 \end{cases}$ c. $\begin{cases} x \geq -2 \\ y < -3 \end{cases}$ d. $\begin{cases} x < -3 \\ y \geq -2 \end{cases}$

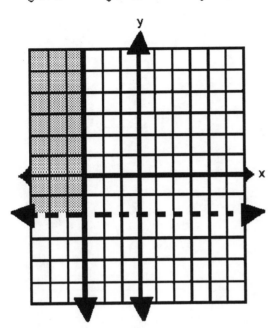

55. Which system of inequalities is graphed here?

a. $\begin{cases} x - y \leq 1 \\ x < -3 \end{cases}$ b. $\begin{cases} x - y < 1 \\ x < -3 \end{cases}$ c. $\begin{cases} x - y \geq 1 \\ x > -3 \end{cases}$ d. $\begin{cases} x - y \leq 1 \\ y > -3 \end{cases}$

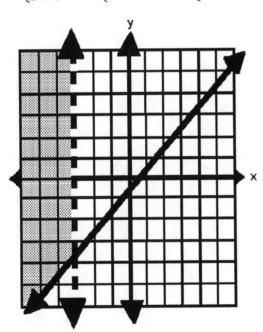

56. Which system of inequalities is graphed here?

a. $\begin{cases} 4x + 2y < 8 \\ y > 2 \end{cases}$
b. $\begin{cases} 4x + 2y < 8 \\ y \geq 2 \end{cases}$
c. $\begin{cases} 4x + 2y \leq 8 \\ y \geq 2 \end{cases}$
d. $\begin{cases} 4x + 2y < 8 \\ x \geq 2 \end{cases}$

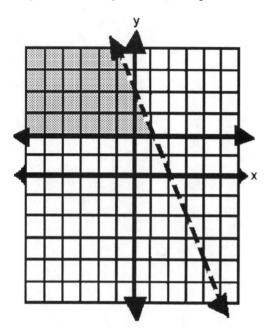

57. Which system of inequalities is graphed here?

a. $\begin{cases} y > 2x + 1 \\ -x + y \leq 5 \end{cases}$
b. $\begin{cases} y > 2x + 1 \\ -x + y < 5 \end{cases}$
c. $\begin{cases} y \geq 2x + 1 \\ -x + y < 5 \end{cases}$
d. $\begin{cases} y \geq 2x + 1 \\ -x + y \leq 5 \end{cases}$

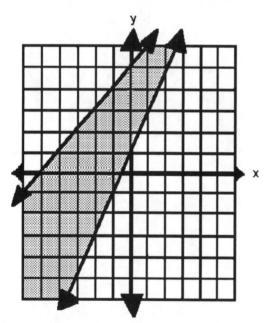

58. A plane flies 1200 miles against the wind in 3 hours. The same trip takes 2 hours with the wind. If x is the speed of the plane with no wind and y is the speed of the wind, which of the following systems of equations could be used to find the speed of the plane with no wind and the speed of the wind?

a. $\begin{cases} 3x - y = 1200 \\ 2x + y = 1200 \end{cases}$
b. $\begin{cases} 2x - y = 1200 \\ 3x + y = 1200 \end{cases}$

c. $\begin{cases} 3(x - y) = 1200 \\ 2(x + y) = 1200 \end{cases}$
d. $\begin{cases} 2(x - y) = 1200 \\ 3(x + y) = 1200 \end{cases}$

24

59. In a coin bank there are 35 quarters and dimes worth a total of $6.50. If q is the number of quarters and d is the number of dimes, which of the following systems of equations could be used to solve for the number of quarters and dimes in the bank?

a. $\begin{cases} q + d = 35 \\ 25q + 10d = 6.50 \end{cases}$ b. $\begin{cases} q + d = 35 \\ 10q + 25d = 650 \end{cases}$

c. $\begin{cases} q + d = 650 \\ 25q + 10d = 35 \end{cases}$ d. $\begin{cases} q + d = 35 \\ 25q + 10d = 650 \end{cases}$

60. A 20% acid solution will be mixed with a 50% acid solution to make 80 ounces of a 45% acid solution. If x is the number of ounces of 20% solution and y is the number of ounces of 50% solution, which of the following systems of equations could be used to solve for the number of ounces of each solution?

a. $\begin{cases} x + y = 80 \\ 0.20x + 0.50y = 0.45(80) \end{cases}$ b. $\begin{cases} x + y = 80 \\ 0.20x + 0.50y = 0.45 \end{cases}$

c. $\begin{cases} x + y = 0.45(80) \\ 0.20x + 0.50y = 0.45 \end{cases}$ d. $\begin{cases} x + y = 80 \\ 20x + 50y = 0.45(80) \end{cases}$

61. A mother is 25 years older than her daughter. In 15 years the mother will be twice as old as her daughter. If m is the mother's age now and d is the daughter's age now, which of the following systems of equations could be used to solve for the ages of the mother and daughter now?

a. $\begin{cases} d = m + 25 \\ d + 15 = 2(m + 15) \end{cases}$ b. $\begin{cases} m = d + 25 \\ m + 15 = 2(d + 15) \end{cases}$

c. $\begin{cases} m = d + 15 \\ m + 25 + 2(d + 25) \end{cases}$ d. $\begin{cases} m = d + 15 \\ m - 25 = 2(d - 25) \end{cases}$

62. The band sold 15 adult tickets and 40 student tickets to their first concert. The band then sold 25 adult tickets and 50 student tickets to their second concert. The band made $320 at their first concert and $450 at their second concert. If x is the price of an adult ticket and y is the price of a student ticket, which of the following systems of equations could be used to solve for the price of an adult ticket and a student ticket?

a. $\begin{cases} 15x + 40y = 450 \\ 25x + 50y = 320 \end{cases}$ b. $\begin{cases} 15x + 25y = 450 \\ 40x + 50y = 320 \end{cases}$

c. $\begin{cases} 15x + 40y = 320 \\ 25x + 50y = 450 \end{cases}$ d. $\begin{cases} 15x - 40y = 320 \\ 25x - 50y = 450 \end{cases}$

63. The sum of two angles is $65°$. The larger angle is $5°$ more than twice the measure of the smaller angle. If x is the measure of the larger angle and y is the measure of the smaller angle, which of the following systems of equations could be used to solve for each of the angles?

a. $\begin{cases} x + y = 65 \\ x = 2y - 5 \end{cases}$ b. $\begin{cases} x + y = 65 \\ x = 5y + 2 \end{cases}$ c. $\begin{cases} x - y = 65 \\ x = 2y + 5 \end{cases}$ d. $\begin{cases} x + y = 65 \\ x = 2y + 5 \end{cases}$

64. The perimeter of a rectangle is 50 meters. The length of the rectangle is 5 meters longer than 4 times the width of the rectangle. If l is the length and w is the width, which of the following systems of equations could be used to find the length and width of the rectangle?

a. $\begin{cases} l + w = 50 \\ l = 5 + 4w \end{cases}$ b. $\begin{cases} 2l + 2w = 50 \\ l = 5 + 4w \end{cases}$ c. $\begin{cases} l + w = 50 \\ w = 5 + 4l \end{cases}$ d. $\begin{cases} 2l + 2w = 50 \\ w = 5 + 4l \end{cases}$

SHORT ANSWER. Write the answer in the space provided.

65. Find the slope of the line graphed here.

_____

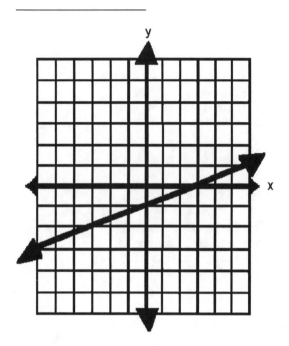

66. Find the slope of the line graphed here.

_____

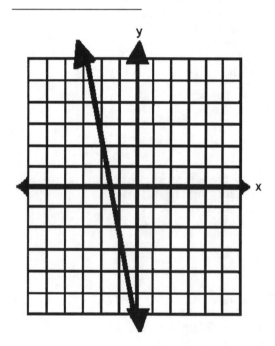

67. Find the slope of the line graphed here.

_____

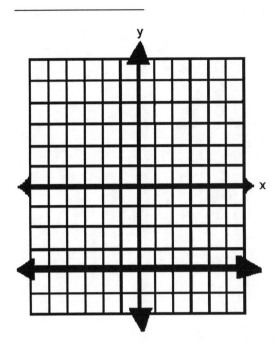

68. Find the slope of the line through the points (-2, 1) and (3, 21).

_____

69. Find the slope of the line through the points (8, 5) and (6, 9).

_____

70. Find the slope of the line through the points (2, -5) and (11, 2).

_____

71. Find the slope of the line through the points (4, 9) and (12, 6).

_____

72. Graph $y = \frac{2}{3}x + 2$.

73. Graph $y = \frac{-3}{4}x + 3$.

74. Find the x-intercept and the y-intercept of the line with the equation $-3x + 4y = 12$. Graph the line.

_____

75. Find the x-intercept and the y-intercept of the line with the equation $5x - 4y = 20$. Graph the line.

_____

76. Write $4x + 7y = 28$ in slope-intercept form. State the slope of the line.

_____

77. Write the equation of the line with a slope of $\frac{3}{5}$ and through the point $(0, 8)$.

_____

78. Write the equation of the line through the points $(1, 4)$ and $(-2, 13)$.

_____

79. Determine whether $(5, -3)$ is a solution to this system of equations:
$$\begin{cases} -3x + y = -18 \\ 4x - y = 17 \end{cases}$$

_____

80. Determine whether $(4, 5)$ is a solution to this system of equations:
$$\begin{cases} 3x - 6y = -18 \\ -5x + 2y = -10 \end{cases}$$

_____

81. Solve by graphing: $\begin{cases} 3x + y = 6 \\ 3x - 3y = -6 \end{cases}$

82. Solve by graphing: $\begin{cases} y = {}^-3x + 3 \\ y = \frac{1}{2}x - 4 \end{cases}$

83. Find the solution to the system of equations graphed.

_____

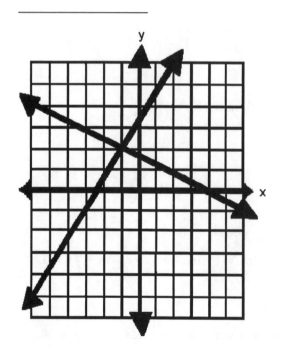

84. Find the solution to the system of equations graphed.

_____

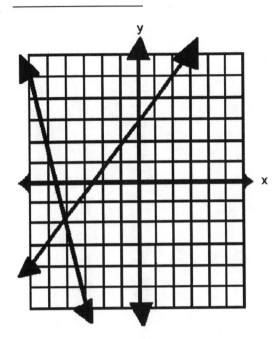

85. Find the solution to the system of equations graphed.

_____

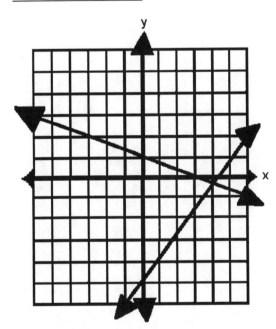

86. Solve by graphing: $\begin{cases} y = 3x \\ 4x + 4y = -16 \end{cases}$.

87. Solve by graphing: $\begin{cases} 3x + y = 4 \\ 2x - y = 6 \end{cases}$.

88. Solve by using the substitution method: $\begin{cases} -5x + y = 16 \\ 3x + 2y = 6 \end{cases}$.

_____

89. Solve by using the substitution method: $\begin{cases} -3x - 2y = -10 \\ x + 5y = -27 \end{cases}$.

_____

90. Solve by using the substitution method: $\begin{cases} 3x = y - 8 \\ -2x + 3y = -18 \end{cases}$.

_____

91. Solve by using the substitution method: $\begin{cases} 4x = 2y + 23 \\ x - 6y = 3 \end{cases}$.

_____

92. Solve by using the substitution method: $\begin{cases} 6x = y + 6 \\ -2y = 3x + 7 \end{cases}$.

_____

93. Solve by using the elimination method: $\begin{cases} -4x + 3y = 36 \\ 4x - 5y = -44 \end{cases}$.

_____

94. Solve by using the elimination method: $\begin{cases} 7x - 4y = 7 \\ 5x - 4y = -3 \end{cases}$.

_____

95. Solve by using the elimination method: $\begin{cases} 6x + y = 17 \\ 5x - 4y = 48 \end{cases}$.

_____

96. Solve by using the elimination method: $\begin{cases} 9x + 2y = -39 \\ 3x - 5y = 21 \end{cases}$.

_____

97. Solve by using the elimination method: $\begin{cases} 5x + 4y = 61 \\ 6x - 5y = 34 \end{cases}$.

_____

98. Solve by using the elimination method: $\begin{cases} 6x - 8y = -37 \\ -8x + 3y = 11 \end{cases}$.

_____

99. Solve by using the elimination method: $\begin{cases} 4x = 5y + 30 \\ 3x - 8y = 14 \end{cases}$.

_____

100. Determine whether the system is dependent, independent, or inconsistent.

_____

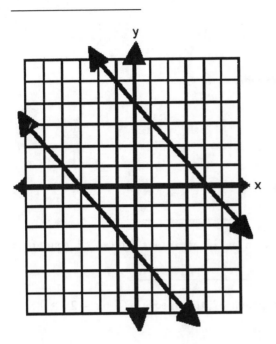

101. Determine whether the system is dependent, independent, or inconsistent.

_____

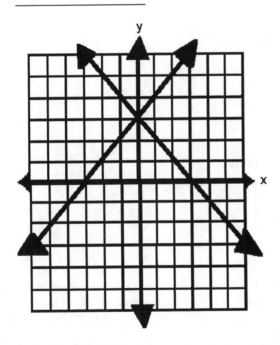

102. Determine whether the system is dependent, independent, or inconsistent.
$$\begin{cases} 3x - y = 4 \\ -9x + 3y = -12 \end{cases}$$

_____

103. Determine whether the system is dependent, independent, or inconsistent.
$$\begin{cases} 5x - 2y = 4 \\ 8x - 3y = 9 \end{cases}$$

_____

104. Determine whether the system is dependent, independent, or inconsistent.
$$\begin{cases} 9x - 6y = 12 \\ 3x - 2y = -9 \end{cases}$$

_____

105. Compare the slopes and y-intercepts of the lines in a dependent system of equations.

_____

106. Compare the slopes and y-intercepts of the lines in an inconsistent system of equations.

_____

107. Write the equation of the boundary line for the graph of the inequality $6x - 2y \geq 8$.

_____

108. Graph $2x - 6y \geq 12$.

109. Graph $y < -2x - 1$.

110. Graph the common solution to the system of inequalities.
$$\begin{cases} x > 2 \\ y \leq -3 \end{cases}$$

111. Graph the common solution to the system of inequalities.
$$\begin{cases} y \leq 2x + 4 \\ y < -3 \end{cases}$$

112. Graph the common solution to the system of inequalities.
$$\begin{cases} x + 2y < 2 \\ x \geq 2 \end{cases}$$

113. Graph the common solution to the system of inequalities.
$$\begin{cases} y \leq 3x \\ x - y \leq 3 \end{cases}$$

114. A plane flies 1200 miles against the wind in 4 hours. The same trip takes 3 hours with the wind. Using x as the speed of the plane with no wind and y as the speed of the wind, write a system of equations to represent the problem. Find the speed of the plane with no wind and the speed of the wind.

_____

_____

115. In a coin bank there are 125 quarters and dimes worth a total of $24.50. Using q as the number of quarters and d as the number of dimes, write a system of equations to represent the problem. How many quarters and how many dimes are in the bank?

_____

_____

116. A 40% acid solution will be mixed with an 80% acid solution to make 80 ounces of a 50% acid solution. Using x as the number of ounces of 40% solution and y as the number of ounces of 80% solution, write a system of equations to represent the problem. How many ounces of each solution should be used?

_____

_____

117. A mother is 24 years older than her daughter. In 6 years, the mother will be 3 times as old as her daughter. Using m as the mother's age now and d as the daughter's age now, write a system of equations to represent the problem. How old are the mother and daughter now?

_____

_____

118. The volleyball team sold 30 adult tickets and 20 student tickets to their first game. The team then sold 50 adult tickets and 40 student tickets to their second game. If the team made $290 at their first game and $510 at their second game, how much are adult tickets and how much are student tickets? Using x as the price of an adult ticket and y as the price of a student ticket, write and solve a system of equations to represent the problem.

_____

_____

119. The sum of two angles is 180°. The larger angle is 20° less than 7 times the measure of the smaller angle. Using x as the measure of the larger angle and y as the measure of the smaller angle, write a system of equations to represent the problem. How large are the angles?

_____

120. The perimeter of a rectangle is 60 meters. If the length of the rectangle is 2 meters longer than 3 times the width of the rectangle, find the length and width of the rectangle. Using l as the length and w as the width, write and solve a system of equations to represent the problem.

_____

_____

1. Answer: a   Section: 1   Objective: 1b

2. Answer: a   Section: 2   Objective: 2a

3. Answer: b   Section: 3   Objective: 3b

4. Answer: a   Section: 4   Objective: 4b

5. Answer: b   Section: 5   Objective: 5a

6. Answer: b   Section: 6   Objective: 6a

7. Answer: a   Section: 7   Objective: 7c

8. Answer: b   Section: 8   Objective: 8a

9. Answer:
   c. $\frac{1}{4}$

   Section: 1   Objective: 1a

10. Answer: a. -2   Section: 1   Objective: 1a

11. Answer: b. 0   Section: 1   Objective: 1a

12. Answer: c. 3   Section: 1   Objective: 1b

13. Answer: a. -4   Section: 1   Objective: 1b

14. Answer:
    c. $\frac{2}{3}$

    Section: 1   Objective: 1b

15. Answer:
    b. $\frac{-3}{5}$

    Section: 1   Objective: 1b

16. Answer: d. slope 3; y-intercept (0, -5)   Section: 2   Objective: 2a

17. Answer: b. $y = 4x + 8$ Section: 2   Objective: 2a

18. Answer: d. (12, 0); (0, -9)   Section: 2   Objective: 2a

19. Answer: b. (-8, 0); (0, 20) Section: 2 Objective: 2a

20. Answer: a. -2 Section: 2 Objective: 2a

21. Answer:

b. $\dfrac{6}{5}$

Section: 2 Objective: 2a

22. Answer: c. $y = 2x + 5$ Section: 2 Objective: 2a

23. Answer: c. (3, -2) Section: 3 Objective: 3a

24. Answer: b. (-2, 5) Section: 3 Objective: 3a

25. Answer: d. (-3, -1) Section: 3 Objective: 3a

26. Answer: b. (3, -1) Section: 3 Objective: 3b

27. Answer: c. (-1, -2) Section: 3 Objective: 3b

28. Answer: a. (0, 3) Section: 3 Objective: 3b

29. Answer: d. (-4, 0) Section: 3 Objective: 3b

30. Answer: c. $x = 2$, $y = -5$ Section: 4 Objective: 4b

31. Answer: a. $x = -4$, $y = -5$ Section: 4 Objective: 4b

32. Answer: b. $x = 3$, $y = -6$ Section: 4 Objective: 4b

33. Answer:

d. $x = -5$, $y = \dfrac{2}{3}$

Section: 4 Objective: 4b

34. Answer:

d. $x = \dfrac{-3}{4}$, $y = 6$

Section: 4 Objective: 4b

35. Answer:

c. $x = -4$, $y = \dfrac{-1}{2}$

Section: 4 Objective: 4b

36. Answer: d. $x = 2$, $y = 6$ Section: 4 Objective: 4b

37. Answer: c. $x = 5$, $y = -4$ Section: 5 Objective: 5a

38. Answer: b. $x = -3$, $y = 7$ Section: 5 Objective: 5a

39. Answer: d. $x = -4$, $y = -3$ Section: 5 Objective: 5a

40. Answer:
c. $x = \frac{1}{2}$, $y = \frac{1}{3}$

Section: 5 Objective: 5a

41. Answer:
b. $x = -2$, $y = \frac{3}{4}$

Section: 5 Objective: 5a

42. Answer: a. $x = -9$, $y = 6$ Section: 5 Objective: 5a

43. Answer:
c. $x = \frac{1}{3}$, $y = \frac{3}{4}$

Section: 5 Objective: 5a

44. Answer: c. inconsistent Section: 6 Objective: 6a

45. Answer: a. independent Section: 6 Objective: 6a

46. Answer: a. independent Section: 6 Objective: 6a

47. Answer: b. dependent Section: 6 Objective: 6a

48. Answer: b. The slopes of the lines are the same, and the y-intercepts of the lines are different.
Section: 6 Objective: 6b

49. Answer: a. The slopes and the y-intercepts of the lines are the same. Section: 6
Objective: 6b

50. Answer: c. $y = -3x + 1$ Section: 6 Objective: 6b

51. Answer: c. $3x + 4y = 12$ Section: 7 Objective: 7a

52. Answer: c. $y \leq x - 2$ Section: 7 Objective: 7b

53. Answer: a. $y > -2x + 4$ Section: 7 Objective: 7b

54. Answer:
b. $\begin{cases} x \leq -3 \\ y > -2 \end{cases}$

Section: 7 Objective: 7c

55. Answer:

a. $\begin{cases} x - y \le 1 \\ x < -3 \end{cases}$

Section: 7 Objective: 7c

56. Answer:

b. $\begin{cases} 4x + 2y < 8 \\ y \ge 2 \end{cases}$

Section: 7 Objective: 7c

57. Answer:

d. $\begin{cases} y \ge 2x + 1 \\ -x + y \le 5 \end{cases}$

Section: 7 Objective: 7c

58. Answer:

c. $\begin{cases} 3(x - y) = 1200 \\ 2(x + y) = 1200 \end{cases}$

Section: 8 Objective: 8a

59. Answer:

d. $\begin{cases} q + d = 35 \\ 25q + 10d = 650 \end{cases}$

Section: 8 Objective: 8a

60. Answer:

a. $\begin{cases} x + y = 80 \\ 0.20x + 0.50y = 0.45(80) \end{cases}$

Section: 8 Objective: 8a

61. Answer:

b. $\begin{cases} m = d + 25 \\ m + 15 = 2(d + 15) \end{cases}$

Section: 8 Objective: 8a

62. Answer:

c. $\begin{cases} 15x + 40y = 320 \\ 25x + 50y = 450 \end{cases}$

Section: 8 Objective: 8a

63. Answer:

d. $\begin{cases} x + y = 65 \\ x = 2y + 5 \end{cases}$

Section: 8 Objective: 8a

64. Answer:

 b. $\begin{cases} 2l + 2w = 50 \\ l = 5 + 4w \end{cases}$

 Section: 8 Objective: 8a

65. Answer:

 $\dfrac{1}{3}$

 Section: 1 Objective: 1a

66. Answer: -4 Section: 1 Objective: 1a

67. Answer: 0 Section: 1 Objective: 1a

68. Answer: 4 Section: 1 Objective: 1b

69. Answer: -2 Section: 1 Objective: 1b

70. Answer:

 $\dfrac{7}{9}$

 Section: 1 Objective: 1b

71. Answer:

 $\dfrac{-3}{8}$

 Section: 1 Objective: 1b

72. Answer:

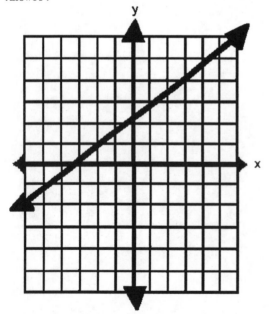

 Section: 2 Objective: 2a

73. Answer:

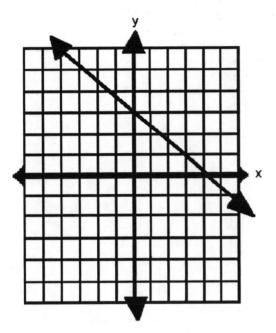

Section: 2 Objective: 2a

74. Answer: (-4,0); (0, 3)

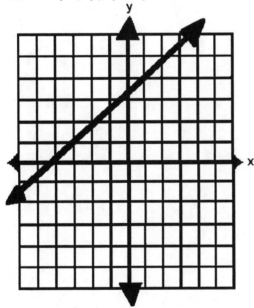

Section: 2 Objective: 2a

75. Answer: (4, 0); (0, -5)

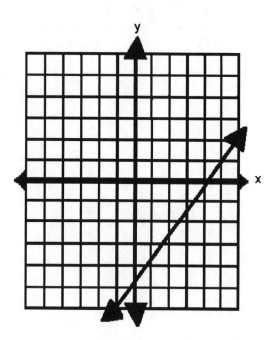

Section: 2 Objective: 2a

76. Answer:
$y = -\frac{4}{7}x + 4$; $-\frac{4}{7}$

Section: 2 Objective: 2a

77. Answer:
$y = \frac{3}{5}x + 8$

Section: 2 Objective: 2a

78. Answer: $y = -3x + 7$ Section: 2 Objective: 2a

79. Answer: It is not a solution. Section: 3 Objective: 3a

80. Answer: It is a solution. Section: 3 Objective: 3a

81. Answer: $x = 1$; $y = 3$

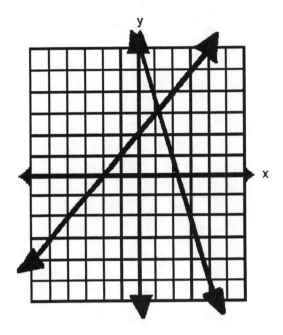

Section: 3   Objective: 3a

82. Answer: $x = 2$; $y = -3$

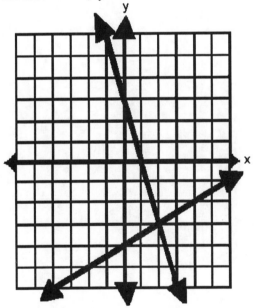

Section: 3   Objective: 3a

83. Answer: (-1, 2)   Section: 3   Objective: 3b

84. Answer: (-4, -2)   Section: 3   Objective: 3b

85. Answer: (4, 0)   Section: 3   Objective: 3b

86. Answer: $x = -1$; $y = -3$

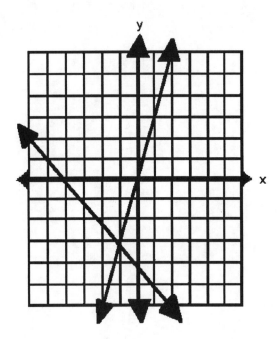

Section: 4   Objective: 4a

87. Answer: $x = 2$; $y = -2$

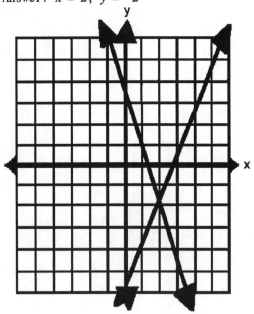

Section: 4   Objective: 4a

88. Answer: $x = -2$; $y = 6$ Section: 4   Objective: 4b

89. Answer: $x = 8$; $y = -7$ Section: 4   Objective: 4b

90. Answer: $x = -6$; $y = -10$ Section: 4   Objective: 4b

91. Answer:
$$x = 6; \ y = \frac{1}{2}$$
Section: 4 Objective: 4b

92. Answer:
$$x = \frac{1}{3}, \ y = -4$$
Section: 4 Objective: 4b

93. Answer: $x = -6$; $y = 4$ Section: 5 Objective: 5a

94. Answer: $x = 5$; $y = 7$ Section: 5 Objective: 5a

95. Answer: $x = 4$; $y = -7$ Section: 5 Objective: 5a

96. Answer: $x = -3$; $y = -6$ Section: 5 Objective: 5a

97. Answer: $x = 9$; $y = 4$ Section: 5 Objective: 5a

98. Answer:
$$x = \frac{1}{2}, \ y = 5$$
Section: 5 Objective: 5a

99. Answer: $x = 10$; $y = 2$ Section: 5 Objective: 5a

100. Answer: inconsistent Section: 6 Objective: 6a

101. Answer: independent Section: 6 Objective: 6a

102. Answer: dependent Section: 6 Objective: 6a

103. Answer: independent Section: 6 Objective: 6a

104. Answer: inconsistent Section: 6 Objective: 6a

105. Answer: The lines have the same slope and y-intercept. Section: 6 Objective: 6b

106. Answer: The lines have the same slope but different y-intercepts. Section: 6
Objective: 6b

107. Answer: $6x - 2y = 8$ Section: 7 Objective: 7a

108. Answer:

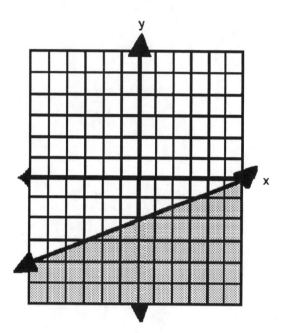

Section: 7 Objective: 7b

109. Answer:

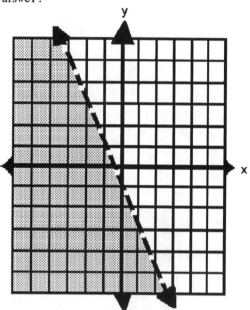

Section: 7 Objective: 7b

44

110. Answer:

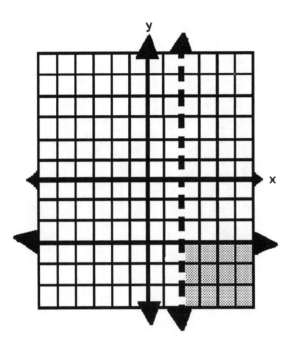

Section: 7   Objective: 7c

111. Answer:

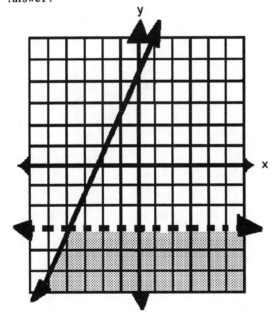

Section: 7   Objective: 7c

112. Answer:

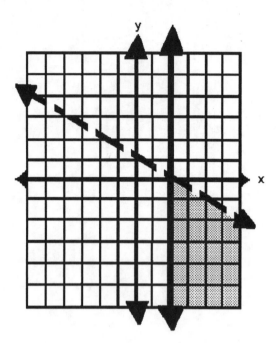

Section: 7 Objective: 7c

113. Answer:

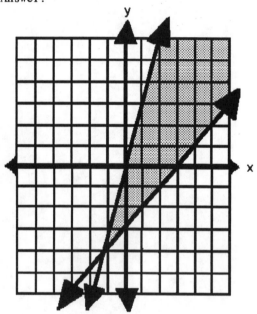

Section: 7 Objective: 7c

114. Answer:
$$\begin{cases} 4(x - y) = 1200 \\ 3(x + y) = 1200 \end{cases};$$
$x = 350$ and $y = 50$; the speed of the plane with no wind is 350 mph, and the speed of the wind is 50 mph.

Section: 8 Objective: 8a

46

115. Answer:

$\begin{cases} q + d = 125 \\ 25q + 10d = 2450 \end{cases}$; $q = 80$ and $d = 45$; 80 quarters and 45 dimes

Section: 8   Objective: 8a

116. Answer:

$\begin{cases} x + y = 80 \\ 0.40x + 0.80y = 0.50(80) \end{cases}$; $x = 60$ and $y = 20$; 60 ounces of the 40% solution and 20 ounces of the 80% solution

Section: 8   Objective: 8a

117. Answer:

$\begin{cases} m = d + 24 \\ m + 6 = 3(d + 6) \end{cases}$; $m = 30$ and $d = 6$; the mother is 30 years old now, and the daughter is 6 years old now.

Section: 8   Objective: 8a

118. Answer:

$\begin{cases} 30x + 20y = 290 \\ 50x + 40y = 510 \end{cases}$; $x = 7$ and $y = 4$; adult tickets cost \$7, and student tickets cost \$4.

Section: 8   Objective: 8a

119. Answer:

$\begin{cases} x + y = 180 \\ x = 7y - 20 \end{cases}$; $x = 155$ and $y = 25$; 155° and 25°

Section: 8   Objective: 8a

120. Answer:

$\begin{cases} 2l + 2w = 60 \\ l = 2 + 3w \end{cases}$; $l = 23$ and $w = 7$; the length is 23 meters, and the width is 7 meters.

Section: 8   Objective: 8a

CHAPTER 3: *Matrices*

QUANTITATIVE COMPARISON

In the space provided, write:
a. if the quantity in Column A is greater than the quantity in Column B;
b. if the quantity in Column B is greater than the quantity in Column A;
c. if the two quantities are equal; or
d. if the relationship cannot be determined from the information given.

Column A	Column B	Answer

1.

| a_{12} in the matrix $A = \begin{bmatrix} 3 & 7 \\ 5 & 9 \end{bmatrix}$ | a_{21} in the matrix $A = \begin{bmatrix} 3 & 7 \\ 5 & 9 \end{bmatrix}$ | _____ |

2.

| The value of x in the equation $\begin{bmatrix} 2 \\ -3 \end{bmatrix} + \begin{bmatrix} x \\ y \end{bmatrix} = \begin{bmatrix} 12 \\ 8 \end{bmatrix}$ | The value of y in the equation $\begin{bmatrix} 2 \\ -3 \end{bmatrix} + \begin{bmatrix} x \\ y \end{bmatrix} = \begin{bmatrix} 12 \\ 8 \end{bmatrix}$ | _____ |

3.

| The product of these matrices $\begin{bmatrix} 2 & 3 \end{bmatrix} \begin{bmatrix} 4 \\ 5 \end{bmatrix}$ | The product of these matrices $\begin{bmatrix} 3 & 6 \end{bmatrix} \begin{bmatrix} 1 \\ 3 \end{bmatrix}$ | _____ |

4.

| AA^{-1} for a $3 \cdot 3$ matrix A | BB^{-1} for a $3 \cdot 3$ matrix B | _____ |

5.

| The value of x in the solution to the matrix equation $\begin{bmatrix} 3 & 1 \\ 2 & 1 \end{bmatrix} \begin{bmatrix} x \\ y \end{bmatrix} = \begin{bmatrix} 5 \\ 4 \end{bmatrix}$ | The value of y in the solution to the matrix equation $\begin{bmatrix} 3 & 1 \\ 2 & 1 \end{bmatrix} \begin{bmatrix} x \\ y \end{bmatrix} = \begin{bmatrix} 5 \\ 4 \end{bmatrix}$ | _____ |

MULTIPLE CHOICE. Circle the letter of the best answer choice.

6. The following matrix shows the numbers of students who are taking the foreign languages offered at Culver High School this year:

Grade 9 10 11 12

$$\begin{array}{c} \text{German} \\ \text{French} \\ \text{Spanish} \end{array} \begin{bmatrix} 24 & 32 & 21 & 35 \\ 16 & 41 & 56 & 34 \\ 32 & 19 & 41 & 40 \end{bmatrix}$$

How many students at Culver High are taking Spanish this year?
a. 32   b. 72   c. 132   d. 391

7. How many students in the 10th grade are taking a foreign language?
a. 32   b. 92   c. 147   d. 391

8. Which of the following is b_{21} in the matrix $B = \begin{bmatrix} 5 & 4 \\ 9 & 0 \\ 1 & 6 \end{bmatrix}$?

a. 9   b. 4   c. 0   d. 6

9. What are the dimensions of the matrix $D = \begin{bmatrix} 1 & 2 & 4 & 8 \\ 2 & 4 & 6 & 8 \end{bmatrix}$?

a. 1 x 2   b. 2 x 4   c. 2 x 1   d. 4 x 2

10. What are the dimensions of the matrix $M = \begin{bmatrix} 2 \\ 2 \\ 2 \\ 2 \end{bmatrix}$?

a. 1 x 2   b. 2 x 1   c. 1 x 4   d. 4 x 1

11. Which of these matrices are equal?

$A = \begin{bmatrix} 2 & 5 \\ 6 & \sqrt{9} \end{bmatrix}$ $B = \begin{bmatrix} 2 & |5| \\ 3^2 & 3 \end{bmatrix}$ $C = \begin{bmatrix} \sqrt{4} & |-5| \\ 9 & 3 \end{bmatrix}$

a. A and B b. A and C c. B and C d. A and B and C

12. Which of these matrices are equal?

$A = \begin{bmatrix} 8 & -3 \\ \sqrt{49} & 4 \end{bmatrix}$ $B = \begin{bmatrix} \sqrt{16} & |-3| \\ 7 & 4 \end{bmatrix}$ $C = \begin{bmatrix} 2^3 & -3 \\ 7 & \sqrt{16} \end{bmatrix}$

a. A and B b. A and C c. B and C d. A and B and C

13. Find $A + B$ for these matrices: $A = \begin{bmatrix} 3 & 5 \\ -7 & -6 \end{bmatrix}$ and $B = \begin{bmatrix} 7 & -9 \\ -4 & -2 \end{bmatrix}$.

a. $\begin{bmatrix} 10 & -4 \\ -3 & -4 \end{bmatrix}$ b. $\begin{bmatrix} 10 & -4 \\ -11 & -8 \end{bmatrix}$ c. $\begin{bmatrix} 10 & 4 \\ -11 & -8 \end{bmatrix}$ d. Not possible

14. Find $A - B$ for these matrices: $A = \begin{bmatrix} 3 & 5 \\ -7 & -6 \end{bmatrix}$ and $B = \begin{bmatrix} 7 & -9 \\ -4 & -2 \end{bmatrix}$.

a. $\begin{bmatrix} 4 & 14 \\ -3 & -4 \end{bmatrix}$ b. $\begin{bmatrix} -4 & 14 \\ 3 & 4 \end{bmatrix}$ c. $\begin{bmatrix} -4 & 14 \\ -3 & -4 \end{bmatrix}$ d. Not possible

15.

Find $A + B$ for these matrices: $A = \begin{bmatrix} 1 & 0 & 2 \\ -1 & 2 & 3 \end{bmatrix}$ and $B = \begin{bmatrix} 4 & 9 \\ 4 & -7 \end{bmatrix}$.

a. $\begin{bmatrix} 5 & 9 \\ 3 & -5 \end{bmatrix}$ b. $\begin{bmatrix} 5 & 11 \\ 3 & -4 \end{bmatrix}$ c. $\begin{bmatrix} 4 & 11 \\ 6 & -4 \end{bmatrix}$ d. Not possible

16.

Find $A + B - C$ for these matrices: $A = \begin{bmatrix} 0 & 1 \\ -4 & 3 \end{bmatrix}$, $B = \begin{bmatrix} 3 & -4 \\ 4 & -1 \end{bmatrix}$, and

$C = \begin{bmatrix} 2 & -1 \\ 0 & -5 \end{bmatrix}$.

a. $\begin{bmatrix} 5 & -4 \\ 0 & -3 \end{bmatrix}$ b. $\begin{bmatrix} 1 & -2 \\ 0 & 7 \end{bmatrix}$ c. $\begin{bmatrix} 1 & -2 \\ 0 & -3 \end{bmatrix}$ d. Not possible

17.

Find $A - B - C$ for these matrices: $A = \begin{bmatrix} 6 & 6 \\ 8 & 4 \\ -5 & 2 \end{bmatrix}$, $B = \begin{bmatrix} 3 & 0 \\ 4 & -3 \\ 1 & -4 \end{bmatrix}$, and

$C = \begin{bmatrix} 0 & 3 \\ 1 & -5 \\ 2 & 2 \end{bmatrix}$.

a. $\begin{bmatrix} 3 & 3 \\ 3 & 12 \\ -8 & 4 \end{bmatrix}$ b. $\begin{bmatrix} 3 & 3 \\ 3 & 12 \\ -2 & -4 \end{bmatrix}$ c. $\begin{bmatrix} 3 & 3 \\ 3 & -4 \\ -2 & -4 \end{bmatrix}$ d. Not possible

18.

If $B = \begin{bmatrix} 7 & 0 \\ -4 & 5 \\ 1 & -2 \end{bmatrix}$, which of the following is $-B$?

a. $-B = \begin{bmatrix} -7 & 0 \\ -4 & -5 \\ -1 & -2 \end{bmatrix}$ b. $-B = \begin{bmatrix} 0 & 7 \\ 5 & -4 \\ -2 & 1 \end{bmatrix}$ c. $-B = \begin{bmatrix} 0 & 0 \\ 0 & 0 \\ 0 & 0 \end{bmatrix}$ d. $-B = \begin{bmatrix} -7 & 0 \\ 4 & -5 \\ -1 & 2 \end{bmatrix}$

19. Which of the following is the identity matrix for addition that will

fit this matrix: $\begin{bmatrix} 4 & 2 \\ -3 & 1 \end{bmatrix}$?

a. $\begin{bmatrix} 1 & 1 \\ 1 & 1 \end{bmatrix}$ b. $\begin{bmatrix} -4 & -2 \\ 3 & -1 \end{bmatrix}$ c. $\begin{bmatrix} 1 & 0 \\ 0 & 1 \end{bmatrix}$ d. $\begin{bmatrix} 0 & 0 \\ 0 & 0 \end{bmatrix}$

20.

Multiply: $3 \begin{bmatrix} 4 & -1 \\ -3 & 0 \\ 2 & 6 \end{bmatrix}$.

a. $\begin{bmatrix} 4 & -1 \\ -9 & 0 \\ 2 & 6 \end{bmatrix}$ b. $\begin{bmatrix} 12 & -3 \\ -9 & 0 \\ 6 & 18 \end{bmatrix}$ c. $\begin{bmatrix} 12 & -1 \\ -9 & 0 \\ 6 & 6 \end{bmatrix}$ d. Not possible

21.

Multiply: $-5\begin{bmatrix} -2 & 1 \\ 5 & 0 \end{bmatrix}$.

a. $\begin{bmatrix} 10 & -5 \\ -25 & 0 \end{bmatrix}$ b. $\begin{bmatrix} 10 & 1 \\ -25 & 0 \end{bmatrix}$ c. $\begin{bmatrix} -10 & 5 \\ 25 & 0 \end{bmatrix}$ d. Not possible

22.

Find $A \times B$ for these matrices: $A = \begin{bmatrix} 3 & 5 \\ 2 & -1 \end{bmatrix}$ and $B = \begin{bmatrix} -3 & 1 \\ 0 & 4 \end{bmatrix}$.

a. $\begin{bmatrix} 0 & 6 \\ 2 & 3 \end{bmatrix}$ b. $\begin{bmatrix} -7 & -16 \\ 8 & -4 \end{bmatrix}$ c. $\begin{bmatrix} -9 & 23 \\ -6 & -2 \end{bmatrix}$ d. Not possible

23.

Find $B \times A$ for these matrices: $A = \begin{bmatrix} 1 & 0 & 3 \\ 2 & 1 & 4 \end{bmatrix}$ and $B = \begin{bmatrix} 1 & 4 \\ 2 & 1 \\ 0 & 3 \end{bmatrix}$.

a. $\begin{bmatrix} 1 & 13 \\ 4 & 21 \end{bmatrix}$ b. $\begin{bmatrix} 9 & 4 & 19 \\ 4 & 1 & 10 \\ 6 & 3 & 12 \end{bmatrix}$ c. $\begin{bmatrix} 2 & 4 & 3 \\ 4 & 2 & 7 \end{bmatrix}$ d. Not possible

24.

Find $A \times B$ for these matrices: $A = \begin{bmatrix} 1 & 0 & 3 \\ 2 & 1 & 4 \end{bmatrix}$ and $B = \begin{bmatrix} 1 & 0 \\ 2 & 3 \end{bmatrix}$.

a. $\begin{bmatrix} 1 & 0 & 3 \\ 8 & 3 & 18 \end{bmatrix}$ b. $\begin{bmatrix} 1 & 0 \\ 8 & 3 \end{bmatrix}$ c. $\begin{bmatrix} 2 & 1 & 6 \\ 4 & 0 & 4 \\ 6 & 3 & 9 \end{bmatrix}$ d. Not possible

25. Which of the following is the identity matrix for multiplication for $\begin{bmatrix} 2 & 5 \\ 8 & 3 \end{bmatrix}$?

a. $\begin{bmatrix} 1 & 1 \\ 1 & 1 \end{bmatrix}$ b. $\begin{bmatrix} 0 & 0 \\ 0 & 0 \end{bmatrix}$ c. $\begin{bmatrix} 0 & 1 \\ 1 & 0 \end{bmatrix}$ d. $\begin{bmatrix} 1 & 0 \\ 0 & 1 \end{bmatrix}$

26.

Multiply: $\begin{bmatrix} 1 & 0 \\ 0 & 1 \end{bmatrix}\begin{bmatrix} 2 & 3 \\ 4 & 5 \end{bmatrix}$.

a. $\begin{bmatrix} 2 & 0 \\ 0 & 5 \end{bmatrix}$ b. $\begin{bmatrix} 0 & 0 \\ 0 & 0 \end{bmatrix}$ c. $\begin{bmatrix} 2 & 3 \\ 4 & 5 \end{bmatrix}$ d. $\begin{bmatrix} -2 & -3 \\ -4 & -5 \end{bmatrix}$

27.

Find the inverse matrix for multiplication for this matrix: $\begin{bmatrix} 2 & 3 \\ 3 & 5 \end{bmatrix}$.

a. $\begin{bmatrix} 1 & 0 \\ 0 & 1 \end{bmatrix}$ b. $\begin{bmatrix} 5 & -3 \\ -3 & 2 \end{bmatrix}$ c. $\begin{bmatrix} -2 & -3 \\ -3 & -5 \end{bmatrix}$ d. There is no inverse.

28.
Find the inverse matrix for multiplication for this matrix: $\begin{bmatrix} 2 & 5 \\ 3 & 7 \end{bmatrix}$.

a. $\begin{bmatrix} -7 & 5 \\ 3 & -2 \end{bmatrix}$ b. $\begin{bmatrix} -1 & 0 \\ 0 & -1 \end{bmatrix}$ c. $\begin{bmatrix} 5 & -2 \\ -7 & 3 \end{bmatrix}$ d. There is no inverse.

29.
Find the inverse matrix for multiplication for this matrix: $\begin{bmatrix} 5 & 3 \\ 6 & 4 \end{bmatrix}$.

a. $\begin{bmatrix} 2 & 1.5 \\ 3 & 2.5 \end{bmatrix}$ b. $\begin{bmatrix} 2 & -1.5 \\ -3 & 2.5 \end{bmatrix}$ c. $\begin{bmatrix} -2 & 1.5 \\ 3 & -2.5 \end{bmatrix}$ d. There is no inverse.

30.
Find the inverse matrix for multiplication for this matrix: $\begin{bmatrix} 3 & 6 \\ 2 & 4 \end{bmatrix}$.

a. $\begin{bmatrix} -3 & -6 \\ -2 & -4 \end{bmatrix}$ b. $\begin{bmatrix} 4 & -6 \\ -2 & 3 \end{bmatrix}$ c. $\begin{bmatrix} -4 & 6 \\ 2 & -3 \end{bmatrix}$ d. There is no inverse.

31. Which of the following matrices has no inverse matrix for multiplication?

a. $\begin{bmatrix} 4 & 7 \\ 3 & 5 \end{bmatrix}$ b. $\begin{bmatrix} 7 & 9 \\ 4 & 5 \end{bmatrix}$ c. $\begin{bmatrix} 10 & -5 \\ 4 & 2 \end{bmatrix}$ d. $\begin{bmatrix} -6 & -3 \\ 8 & 4 \end{bmatrix}$

32.
Find the inverse matrix for multiplication for this matrix: $\begin{bmatrix} 1 & 0 & 2 \\ 0 & 1 & 1 \\ 0 & 1 & 0 \end{bmatrix}$.

a. $\begin{bmatrix} 1 & 0 & 0 \\ 0 & 1 & 0 \\ 0 & 0 & 1 \end{bmatrix}$ b. $\begin{bmatrix} 1 & -2 & 2 \\ 0 & 0 & 1 \\ 0 & 1 & -1 \end{bmatrix}$ c. $\begin{bmatrix} -1 & 0 & -2 \\ 0 & -1 & -1 \\ 0 & -1 & 0 \end{bmatrix}$ d. There is no inverse.

33. Find the inverse matrix for multiplication for this matrix:
$\begin{bmatrix} 1 & 0 & 3 \\ 0 & 1 & 0 \\ 0 & 4 & 1 \end{bmatrix}$.

a. $\begin{bmatrix} 1 & 12 & -3 \\ 0 & 1 & 0 \\ 0 & -4 & 1 \end{bmatrix}$ b. $\begin{bmatrix} 1 & 12 & 3 \\ 0 & 1 & 0 \\ 0 & 4 & -1 \end{bmatrix}$ c. $\begin{bmatrix} -1 & 0 & 0 \\ 0 & -1 & 0 \\ 0 & 0 & -1 \end{bmatrix}$ d. There is no inverse.

34. Which of the following is the coefficient matrix for this system of equations: $\begin{cases} 2x + 5y = 8 \\ 4x - 7y = 2 \end{cases}$?

a. $\begin{bmatrix} 2 & 4 \\ 5 & -7 \end{bmatrix}$ b. $\begin{bmatrix} 2 & 5 \\ 4 & -7 \end{bmatrix}$ c. $\begin{bmatrix} 2 & 4 & 8 \\ 5 & -7 & 2 \end{bmatrix}$ d. $\begin{bmatrix} 2 & 5 & 8 \\ 4 & -7 & 2 \end{bmatrix}$

35. Represent this system of equations in matrix equation form:
$$\begin{cases} 5x = 3y + 9 \\ 4y = 2x - 6 \end{cases}$$

a. $\begin{bmatrix} 5 & 3 \\ 4 & 2 \end{bmatrix} \begin{bmatrix} x \\ y \end{bmatrix} = \begin{bmatrix} 9 \\ -6 \end{bmatrix}$ b. $\begin{bmatrix} 5 & -3 \\ 4 & -2 \end{bmatrix} \begin{bmatrix} x \\ y \end{bmatrix} = \begin{bmatrix} 9 \\ -6 \end{bmatrix}$

c. $\begin{bmatrix} 5 & -3 \\ -2 & 4 \end{bmatrix} \begin{bmatrix} x \\ y \end{bmatrix} = \begin{bmatrix} 9 \\ -6 \end{bmatrix}$ d. $\begin{bmatrix} 5 & -2 \\ 4 & -3 \end{bmatrix} \begin{bmatrix} x \\ y \end{bmatrix} = \begin{bmatrix} 9 \\ -6 \end{bmatrix}$

36. Use matrices to solve this system of equations: $\begin{cases} 2x + 3y = 11 \\ 3x + 5y = 19 \end{cases}$
    a. $x = 2$; $y = 5$ b. $x = 2$; $y = -5$ c. $x = -2$; $y = 5$ d. $x = -2$; $y = -5$

37. Use matrices to solve this system of equations: $\begin{cases} 8x - 3y = 41 \\ 5x - 2y = 26 \end{cases}$
    a. $x = -4$; $y = -3$ b. $x = 4$; $y = -3$ c. $x = -4$; $y = 3$ d. $x = 4$; $y = 3$

38. Represent this system of equations in matrix equation form:
$$\begin{cases} 5x + 3y + 2z = 9 \\ 4x - 2y + 6z = 7. \\ 2x + 5y + z = 5 \end{cases}$$

a. $\begin{bmatrix} 5 & 4 & 2 \\ 3 & -2 & 5 \\ 2 & 6 & 1 \end{bmatrix} \begin{bmatrix} x \\ y \\ z \end{bmatrix} = \begin{bmatrix} 9 \\ 7 \\ 5 \end{bmatrix}$ b. $\begin{bmatrix} 5 & 3 & 2 \\ 4 & -2 & 6 \\ 2 & 5 & 1 \end{bmatrix} \begin{bmatrix} x \\ y \\ z \end{bmatrix} = \begin{bmatrix} 9 \\ 7 \\ 5 \end{bmatrix}$

c. $\begin{bmatrix} 5 & 3 & 2 \\ 4 & -2 & 6 \\ 2 & 5 & 0 \end{bmatrix} \begin{bmatrix} x \\ y \\ z \end{bmatrix} = \begin{bmatrix} 9 \\ 7 \\ 5 \end{bmatrix}$ d. $\begin{bmatrix} -5 & 3 & 2 \\ 4 & 2 & 6 \\ 2 & 5 & 0 \end{bmatrix} \begin{bmatrix} x \\ y \\ z \end{bmatrix} = \begin{bmatrix} 9 \\ 7 \\ 5 \end{bmatrix}$

39. Use matrices to solve this system of equations: $\begin{cases} 2x - y + 2z = 1 \\ x + 3y + 4z = 14. \\ 2x + y - 5z = 0 \end{cases}$

    a. $x = 0$; $y = 3$; $z = 2$ b. $x = 1$; $y = -3$; $z = -2$
    c. $x = 1$; $y = 3$; $z = 1$ d. $x = -1$; $y = 3$; $z = -1$

40. Use matrices to solve this system of equations: $\begin{cases} 2x + 3y + z = -4 \\ 4x - 3y + 2z = 10 \\ 2x + 4y - 3z = -14 \end{cases}$

    a. $x = 0$; $y = 2$; $z = -2$ b. $x = 1$; $y = -2$; $z = 2$
    c. $x = 1$; $y = 2$; $z = -2$ d. $x = 0$; $y = -2$; $z = 2$

SHORT ANSWER. Write the answer in the space provided.

41. A hockey league has 4 teams: the Eagles, the Tigers, the Sharks, and the Lions. Last year the Eagles won 8 games, lost 7 games, and tied 1 game. Last year the Tigers won 7 games, lost 8 games, and tied 1 game. Last year the Sharks won 5 games, lost 10 games, and tied 1 game. Last year the Lions won 10 games, lost 5 games, and tied 1 game. Using the teams as rows, form matrix A to show the order in which the teams finished last year. What does a_{32} mean in this case?

_____

42. The drama club put on performances of the spring play on Friday, Saturday, and Sunday. On Friday the club sold 65 adult tickets, 98 student tickets, and 15 child tickets. On Saturday the club sold 85 adult tickets, 73 student tickets, and 24 child tickets. On Sunday the club sold 72 adult tickets, 83 student tickets, and 20 child tickets. Using the days as rows, form matrix P to show the ticket sales for the spring play.

_____

43.

Find d_{23} in this matrix: $D = \begin{bmatrix} 1 & 3 & 5 \\ 2 & 4 & 6 \\ 7 & 8 & 9 \end{bmatrix}$.

_____

44.

What are the dimensions of the matrix $C = \begin{bmatrix} 5 & 4 \\ 9 & 0 \\ 1 & 6 \end{bmatrix}$?

_____

45.

What are the dimensions of the matrix $A = \begin{bmatrix} 0 & 1 & 2 & 3 \\ 4 & 5 & 6 & 7 \end{bmatrix}$?

_____

46. Matrices A and B are equal. Find the values of x and y.

$A = \begin{bmatrix} 9 & 2x - 5 \\ 24 & -15 \end{bmatrix}$ $B = \begin{bmatrix} 9 & 4x + 9 \\ 24 & y - 8 \end{bmatrix}$

_____

47. Matrices A and B are equal. Find the values of x and y.

$A = \begin{bmatrix} 5 & 5x - 6 & -10 \\ 4 & 9 & -5y \end{bmatrix}$ $B = \begin{bmatrix} 5 & -3x + 10 & -10 \\ 4 & 9 & y + 12 \end{bmatrix}$

_____

48.

Find $A - B$ for these matrices: $A = \begin{bmatrix} 1 & 7 & 0 \\ -2 & -5 & 3 \end{bmatrix}$ and $B = \begin{bmatrix} 0 & -2 & -5 \\ -6 & 4 & 3 \end{bmatrix}$.

_____

49.

Find $A + B$ for these matrices: $A = \begin{bmatrix} 1 & 4 & 0 \\ 6 & 6 & 7 \end{bmatrix}$ and $B = \begin{bmatrix} 2 & -6 \\ 0 & 4 \end{bmatrix}$.

_____

50.

Find $A - B + C$ for these matrices: $A = \begin{bmatrix} 3 & -4 \\ 0 & 5 \end{bmatrix}$, $B = \begin{bmatrix} -2 & 0 \\ 6 & -3 \end{bmatrix}$, and

$C = \begin{bmatrix} 5 & -1 \\ -4 & 2 \end{bmatrix}$.

_____

51.

Find $A - B - C$ for these matrices: $A = \begin{bmatrix} -3 & 0 \\ 0 & 5 \end{bmatrix}$, $B = \begin{bmatrix} 6 & 2 \\ -4 & -3 \end{bmatrix}$, and

$C = \begin{bmatrix} -2 & -5 \\ -1 & 0 \end{bmatrix}$.

_____

52. Find the values of x and y by solving the matrix equation $A + B = C$.

$A = \begin{bmatrix} -3 & 3x + 4 \\ y - 8 & 5 \end{bmatrix}$, $B = \begin{bmatrix} 6 & 2x + 6 \\ -4y & -3 \end{bmatrix}$, $C = \begin{bmatrix} 3 & 25 \\ 13 & 2 \end{bmatrix}$

_____

53. Write the identity matrix for addition that will fit the matrix

$A = \begin{bmatrix} 6 & 6 \\ 8 & 4 \\ -5 & 2 \end{bmatrix}$.

_____

54.

If $A = \begin{bmatrix} 3 & 5 & 0 \\ -6 & 2 & -7 \end{bmatrix}$, find $-A$.

_____

55.

Multiply: $4 \begin{bmatrix} 1 & 0 & 3 \\ -2 & 3 & -5 \end{bmatrix}$.

_____

56.

Multiply: $-7 \begin{bmatrix} -3 & 0 \\ 2 & -5 \end{bmatrix}$.

_____

57.

Find $A \times B$ for these matrices: $A = \begin{bmatrix} 5 & -1 \\ 0 & 4 \end{bmatrix}$ and $B = \begin{bmatrix} 4 & 0 \\ -2 & 3 \end{bmatrix}$.

_____

58.

Find $B \times A$ for these matrices: $A = \begin{bmatrix} 2 & 1 \\ 3 & 5 \\ 0 & 2 \end{bmatrix}$ and $B = \begin{bmatrix} 3 & 1 & 0 \\ 2 & 5 & 1 \end{bmatrix}$

_____

59.

Find $A \times B$ for these matrices: $A = \begin{bmatrix} 1 & 0 & 6 \\ 4 & 1 & 3 \\ 1 & 0 & 4 \end{bmatrix}$ and $B = \begin{bmatrix} 3 & 1 & 0 \\ 2 & 5 & 1 \end{bmatrix}$

_____

60.

Write the identity matrix for multiplication for the matrix $\begin{bmatrix} 1 & 4 & 8 \\ 3 & 1 & 3 \\ 1 & 0 & 7 \end{bmatrix}$.

_____

61.

Multiply: $\begin{bmatrix} 1 & 0 \\ 0 & 1 \end{bmatrix} \begin{bmatrix} 9 & -6 \\ -8 & 21 \end{bmatrix}$.

_____

62.

Find the inverse matrix for multiplication for this matrix: $\begin{bmatrix} 1 & 2 \\ 2 & 5 \end{bmatrix}$.

_____

63.

Find the inverse matrix for multiplication for this matrix: $\begin{bmatrix} 4 & 7 \\ 3 & 5 \end{bmatrix}$.

_____

64.

Find the inverse matrix for multiplication for this matrix: $\begin{bmatrix} 7 & 4 \\ 3 & 2 \end{bmatrix}$.

_____

65.

Find the inverse matrix for multiplication for this matrix: $\begin{bmatrix} 9 & 6 \\ 3 & 2 \end{bmatrix}$.

_____

66.

Find the inverse matrix for multiplication for this matrix: $\begin{bmatrix} 1 & 2 & 1 \\ 0 & 1 & 0 \\ 0 & 3 & 1 \end{bmatrix}$.

_____

67.

Find the inverse matrix for multiplication for this matrix: $\begin{bmatrix} 1 & 0 & 5 \\ 0 & 1 & 3 \\ 0 & 0 & 1 \end{bmatrix}$.

_____

68.

Find the inverse matrix for multiplication for this matrix: $\begin{bmatrix} 1 & 2 & 3 \\ 4 & 5 & 6 \\ 7 & 8 & 9 \end{bmatrix}$.

_____

69. Represent this system of equations in matrix equation form:
$\begin{cases} 3y = 8x + 4 \\ 2x + 8 = 7y \end{cases}$

_____

70. Use matrices to solve this system of equations: $\begin{cases} 4x + 3y = 26 \\ 7x + 5y = 45 \end{cases}$.

_____

71. Use matrices to solve this system of equations: $\begin{cases} 6x + 5y = -8 \\ 5x + 4y = -6 \end{cases}$.

_____

72. Use matrices to solve this system of equations: $\begin{cases} 4x - 3y = -15 \\ -6x + 4y = 22 \end{cases}$.

_____

73. Represent this system of equations in matrix equation form:
$\begin{cases} 3x - 7y + 2z = 6 \\ x + 2y + 8z = 7 \\ 2x + y - 5z = 12 \end{cases}$.

_____

74.

Use matrices to solve this system of equations: $\begin{cases} 5x + 3y + z = 8 \\ 2x + 3y - 2z = -1 \\ 4x - y + 3z = 12 \end{cases}$.

_____

75. At a restaurant Jim ordered 14 sandwiches and 6 drinks for his friends. At the same restaurant Amy ordered 10 sandwiches and 8 drinks for her friends. Jim's order cost $38, and Amy's order cost $29. Using x as the cost of a sandwich and y as the cost of a drink, write a system of equations to represent the problem. Find the cost of a sandwich and the cost of a drink by using matrices.

_____

ANSWERS TO CHAPTER 3

1. Answer: a   Section: 1   Objective: 1b

2. Answer: b   Section: 2   Objective: 2a

3. Answer:
   a

   Section: 3   Objective: 3a

4. Answer: c   Section: 4   Objective: 4a

5. Answer: b   Section: 5   Objective: 5a

6. Answer: c. 132   Section: 1   Objective: 1a

7. Answer: b. 92   Section: 1   Objective: 1a

8. Answer: a. 9   Section: 1   Objective: 1b

9. Answer: b. 2 x 4   Section: 1   Objective: 1b

10. Answer: d. 4 x 1   Section: 1   Objective: 1b

11. Answer: c. *B* and *C*   Section: 1   Objective: 1c

12. Answer: b. *A* and *C*   Section: 1   Objective: 1c

13. Answer:
    b. $\begin{bmatrix} 10 & -4 \\ -11 & -8 \end{bmatrix}$

    Section: 2   Objective: 2a

14. Answer:
    c. $\begin{bmatrix} -4 & 14 \\ -3 & -4 \end{bmatrix}$

    Section: 2   Objective: 2a

15. Answer: d. Not possible   Section: 2   Objective: 2a

16. Answer:
    b. $\begin{bmatrix} 1 & -2 \\ 0 & 7 \end{bmatrix}$

    Section: 2   Objective: 2a

17. Answer:

a. $\begin{bmatrix} 3 & 3 \\ 3 & 12 \\ -8 & 4 \end{bmatrix}$

Section: 2 Objective: 2a

18. Answer:

d. $-B = \begin{bmatrix} -7 & 0 \\ 4 & -5 \\ -1 & 2 \end{bmatrix}$

Section: 2 Objective: 2b

19. Answer:

d. $\begin{bmatrix} 0 & 0 \\ 0 & 0 \end{bmatrix}$

Section: 2 Objective: 2b

20. Answer:

b. $\begin{bmatrix} 12 & -3 \\ -9 & 0 \\ 6 & 18 \end{bmatrix}$

Section: 3 Objective: 3a

21. Answer:

a. $\begin{bmatrix} 10 & -5 \\ -25 & 0 \end{bmatrix}$

Section: 3 Objective: 3a

22. Answer:

c. $\begin{bmatrix} -9 & 23 \\ -6 & -2 \end{bmatrix}$

Section: 3 Objective: 3a

23. Answer:

b. $\begin{bmatrix} 9 & 4 & 19 \\ 4 & 1 & 10 \\ 6 & 3 & 12 \end{bmatrix}$

Section: 3 Objective: 3a

24. Answer: d. Not possible Section: 3 Objective: 3a

25. Answer:

d. $\begin{bmatrix} 1 & 0 \\ 0 & 1 \end{bmatrix}$

Section: 3 Objective: 3b

26. Answer:

c. $\begin{bmatrix} 2 & 3 \\ 4 & 5 \end{bmatrix}$

Section: 3 Objective: 3b

27. Answer:

b. $\begin{bmatrix} 5 & -3 \\ -3 & 2 \end{bmatrix}$

Section: 4 Objective: 4a

28. Answer:

a. $\begin{bmatrix} -7 & 5 \\ 3 & -2 \end{bmatrix}$

Section: 4 Objective: 4a

29. Answer:

b. $\begin{bmatrix} 2 & -1.5 \\ -3 & 2.5 \end{bmatrix}$

Section: 4 Objective: 4a

30. Answer: d. There is no inverse. Section: 4 Objective: 4a

31. Answer:

d. $\begin{bmatrix} -6 & -3 \\ 8 & 4 \end{bmatrix}$

Section: 4 Objective: 4a

32. Answer:

b. $\begin{bmatrix} 1 & -2 & 2 \\ 0 & 0 & 1 \\ 0 & 1 & -1 \end{bmatrix}$

Section: 4 Objective: 4b

33. Answer:

a. $\begin{bmatrix} 1 & 12 & -3 \\ 0 & 1 & 0 \\ 0 & -4 & 1 \end{bmatrix}$

Section: 4 Objective: 4b

34. Answer:

b. $\begin{bmatrix} 2 & 5 \\ 4 & -7 \end{bmatrix}$

Section: 5 Objective: 5a

35. Answer:

c. $\begin{bmatrix} 5 & -3 \\ -2 & 4 \end{bmatrix} \begin{bmatrix} x \\ y \end{bmatrix} = \begin{bmatrix} 9 \\ -6 \end{bmatrix}$

Section: 5 Objective: 5a

36. Answer: c. $x = -2$; $y = 5$ Section: 5 Objective: 5a

37. Answer: b. $x = 4$; $y = -3$ Section: 5 Objective: 5a

38. Answer:

b. $\begin{bmatrix} 5 & 3 & 2 \\ 4 & -2 & 6 \\ 2 & 5 & 1 \end{bmatrix} \begin{bmatrix} x \\ y \\ z \end{bmatrix} = \begin{bmatrix} 9 \\ 7 \\ 5 \end{bmatrix}$

Section: 5 Objective: 5b

39. Answer: c. $x = 1$; $y = 3$; $z = 1$ Section: 5 Objective: 5b

40. Answer: d. $x = 0$; $y = -2$; $z = 2$ Section: 5 Objective: 5b

41. Answer:

$$A = \begin{array}{c} \\ \text{Lions} \\ \text{Eagles} \\ \text{Tigers} \\ \text{Sharks} \end{array} \begin{bmatrix} \text{Won} & \text{Lost} & \text{Tied} \\ 10 & 5 & 1 \\ 8 & 7 & 1 \\ 7 & 8 & 1 \\ 5 & 10 & 1 \end{bmatrix}; \text{ the Tigers lost 8 games last year.}$$

Section: 1 Objective: 1a

42. Answer:

$$P = \begin{array}{c} \\ \text{Friday} \\ \text{Saturday} \\ \text{Sunday} \end{array} \begin{bmatrix} \text{Adult} & \text{Student} & \text{Child} \\ 65 & 98 & 15 \\ 85 & 73 & 24 \\ 72 & 83 & 20 \end{bmatrix}$$

Section: 1 Objective: 1a

43. Answer: 6 Section: 1 Objective: 1b

44. Answer: 3 x 2 Section: 1 Objective: 1b

45. Answer: 2 x 4 Section: 1 Objective: 1b

46. Answer: $x = -7$; $y = -7$ Section: 1 Objective: 1c

47. Answer: $x = 2$; $y = -2$ Section: 1 Objective: 1c

48. Answer:

$$\begin{bmatrix} 1 & 9 & 5 \\ 4 & -9 & 0 \end{bmatrix}$$

Section: 2 Objective: 2a

49. Answer: Not possible Section: 2 Objective: 2a

50. Answer:

$$\begin{bmatrix} 10 & -5 \\ -10 & 10 \end{bmatrix}$$

Section: 2 Objective: 2a

51. Answer:

$$\begin{bmatrix} -7 & 3 \\ 5 & 8 \end{bmatrix}$$

Section: 2 Objective: 2a

52. Answer: $x = 3$; $y = -7$ Section: 2 Objective: 2a

53. Answer:

$$\begin{bmatrix} 0 & 0 \\ 0 & 0 \\ 0 & 0 \end{bmatrix}$$

Section: 2 Objective: 2b

54. Answer:

$$-A = \begin{bmatrix} -3 & -5 & 0 \\ 6 & -2 & 7 \end{bmatrix}$$

Section: 2 Objective: 2b

55. Answer:

$$\begin{bmatrix} 4 & 0 & 12 \\ -8 & 12 & -20 \end{bmatrix}$$

Section: 3 Objective: 3a

56. Answer:

$$\begin{bmatrix} 21 & 0 \\ -14 & 35 \end{bmatrix}$$

Section: 3 Objective: 3a

57. Answer:

$$\begin{bmatrix} 22 & -3 \\ -8 & 12 \end{bmatrix}$$

Section: 3 Objective: 3a

58. Answer:

$$\begin{bmatrix} 9 & 8 \\ 19 & 29 \end{bmatrix}$$

Section: 3 Objective: 3a

59. Answer: Not possible Section: 3 Objective: 3a

60. Answer:

$$\begin{bmatrix} 1 & 0 & 0 \\ 0 & 1 & 0 \\ 0 & 0 & 1 \end{bmatrix}$$

Section: 3 Objective: 3b

61. Answer:

$$\begin{bmatrix} 9 & -6 \\ -8 & 21 \end{bmatrix}$$

Section: 3 Objective: 3b

62. Answer:

$$\begin{bmatrix} 5 & -2 \\ -2 & 1 \end{bmatrix}$$

Section: 4 Objective: 4a

63. Answer:

$$\begin{bmatrix} -5 & 7 \\ 3 & -4 \end{bmatrix}$$

Section: 4 Objective: 4a

64. Answer:

$$\begin{bmatrix} 1 & -2 \\ -1.5 & 3.5 \end{bmatrix}$$

Section: 4 Objective: 4a

65. Answer: There is no inverse. Section: 4 Objective: 4a

66. Answer:

$$\begin{bmatrix} 1 & 1 & -1 \\ 0 & 1 & 0 \\ 0 & -3 & 1 \end{bmatrix}$$

Section: 4 Objective: 4b

67. Answer:

$$\begin{bmatrix} 1 & 0 & -5 \\ 0 & 1 & -3 \\ 0 & 0 & 1 \end{bmatrix}$$

Section: 4 Objective: 4b

68. Answer: There is no inverse. Section: 4 Objective: 4b

69. Answer:

$$\begin{bmatrix} -8 & 3 \\ 2 & -7 \end{bmatrix} \begin{bmatrix} x \\ y \end{bmatrix} = \begin{bmatrix} 4 \\ -8 \end{bmatrix}$$

Section: 5 Objective: 5a

70. Answer: $x = 5$; $y = 2$ Section: 5 Objective: 5a

71. Answer: $x = 2$; $y = -4$ Section: 5 Objective: 5a

72. Answer: $x = -3$; $y = 1$ Section: 5 Objective: 5a

73. Answer:

$$\begin{bmatrix} 3 & -7 & 2 \\ 1 & 2 & 8 \\ 2 & 1 & -5 \end{bmatrix} \begin{bmatrix} x \\ y \\ z \end{bmatrix} = \begin{bmatrix} 6 \\ 7 \\ 12 \end{bmatrix}$$

Section: 5 Objective: 5b

74. Answer: $x = 2$; $y = -1$; $z = 1$ Section: 5 Objective: 5b

75. Answer:
$\begin{cases} 14x + 6y = 38 \\ 10x + 8y = 29 \end{cases}$; $x = 2.5$, $y = 0.5$; sandwiches cost $2.50, and drinks cost $0.50.

Section: 5 Objective: 5b

CHAPTER 4: Probability and Statistics

QUANTITATIVE COMPARISON

In the space provided, write:
a. if the quantity in Column A is greater than the quantity in Column B;
b. if the quantity in Column B is greater than the quantity in Column A;
c. if the two quantities are equal; or
d. if the relationship cannot be determined from the information given.

Column A	Column B	Answer

1.

The theoretical probability of the spinner landing in a region with an even number	The theoretical probability of the spinner landing in a region with an odd number	_____

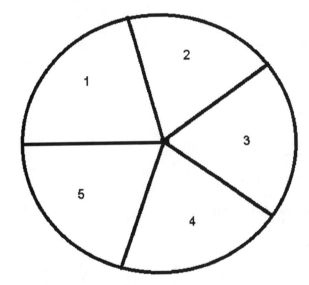

2.

The largest number generated by the command INT(5*RAND) + 8	The largest number generated by the command INT(9*RAND) + 2	_____

3.

Median of 4, 6, 8, 20	Mean of 4, 6, 8, 20	_____

4. The table shows what students are taking in summer school.

	Math	Science
Boys	25	15
Girls	19	21

The number of students taking math	The number of students taking math OR science

_____

5.

The number of ways there are to arrange the letters in the word *bat*, using each letter exactly once	The number of ways there are to arrange the letters in the word *base*, using each letter exactly once

_____

6.

If an integer between 1 and 20 inclusive is drawn at random, the probability that the number is a multiple of 3	If an integer between 1 and 20 inclusive is drawn at random, the probability that the number is a multiple of 5

_____

7.

A number cube is rolled twice. The probability that the result is 5 on the second roll if the result was 5 on the first roll	A number cube is rolled twice. The probability that the result is 5 on the second roll if the result was not 5 on the first roll

_____

MULTIPLE CHOICE. Circle the letter of the best answer choice.

8. Which of the following is the theoretical probability that the spinner will land on 5 when spun?

a. $\frac{1}{5}$ b. $\frac{5}{8}$ c. $\frac{1}{2}$ d. $\frac{1}{8}$

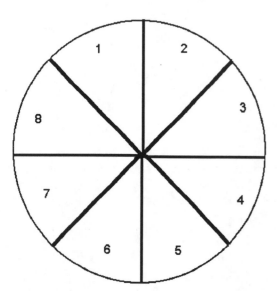

9. Pat flips two coins 12 times with these results: HH, TH, HT, HT, TH, TT, TH, TT, HH, HT, HT, TT. Find the experimental probability in this case that both coins come up heads.

   a. $\frac{1}{2}$ b. $\frac{1}{4}$ c. $\frac{1}{6}$ d. $\frac{1}{8}$

10. Sam rolls two number cubes together 15 times with these results: 6 and 1, 5 and 4, 2 and 4, 3 and 3, 5 and 1, 4 and 4, 1 and 6, 2 and 6, 6 and 6, 4 and 1, 2 and 3, 3 and 6, 1 and 1, 6 and 4, 3 and 5. Find the experimental probability in this case that both number cubes show the same number.

    a. $\frac{1}{2}$ b. $\frac{1}{5}$ c. $\frac{6}{15}$ d. $\frac{4}{15}$

11. A baseball coach keeps track of the number of errors that the team makes in a game. The results are shown in this table.

Errors	0	1	2	3
Frequency	3	9	3	5

    What is the experimental probability that this team will make exactly 1 error in a game?

    a. $\frac{1}{4}$ b. $\frac{9}{20}$ c. $\frac{1}{2}$ d. $\frac{3}{10}$

12. A teacher keeps track of the number of students who are absent from algebra class. The results are shown in this table.

Absent	0	1	2	3	4
Frequency	2	9	7	6	1

    What is the experimental probability that there will be exactly 2 people absent from this class?

    a. $\frac{7}{25}$ b. $\frac{5}{25}$ c. $\frac{1}{5}$ d. $\frac{1}{3}$

13. Which of the following is the output of the command INT(4*RAND) + 2?
    a. 0, 1, 2, 3   b. 2, 3, 4, 5, 6   c. 2, 3, 4   d. 2, 3, 4, 5

14. Which of the following is the output of the command INT(3*RAND) + 4?
    a. 0, 1, 2   b. 3, 4, 5, 6   c. 4, 5, 6   d. 4, 5, 6, 7

15. Which of the following commands will generate this output: 4, 5, 6, 7, 8, 9?
    a. INT(9*RAND) + 4   b. INT(6*RAND) + 4
    c. INT(4*RAND) + 9   d. INT(6*RAND) + 9

16. Which of the following commands will generate this output: 5, 6, 7, 8, 9, 10, 11, 12?
    a. INT(5*RAND) + 8   b. INT(5*RAND) + 8
    c. INT(8*RAND) + 5   d. INT(12*RAND) + 5

17. Which of the following commands could be used to simulate a traffic light?
    a. INT(5*RAND)   b. INT(3*RAND)
    c. INT(5*RAND) + 3   d. INT(4*RAND) + 3

18. Which of the following commands could be used to simulate selecting 1 student out of 30?
    a. INT(RAND) + 1   b. INT(1*RAND) + 30
    c. INT(30*RAND) + 1   d. INT(20*RAND) + 10

19. Which of the following commands could be used to simulate guessing correctly on a multiple-choice question with 5 possible answers?
    a. INT(2*RAND) + 5   b. INT(2*RAND)
    c. INT(3*RAND) + 2   d. INT(5*RAND)

20. A baseball player gets a hit 30% of the time he bats. The player simulates his at-bats by using the random integers 0 through 9, where 0, 1, and 2 represent hits. The player wants to simulate the 15 times at-bat that he expects to get in the next week. Here are the results: 4, 6, 2, 8, 9, 1, 1, 7, 0, 5, 3, 8, 2, 9, 6. How many hits does the simulation predict that the player will get?
    a. 3   b. 4   c. 5   d. 6

21. A softball relief pitcher appears in 60% of the games that her team plays. The player simulates her team's games by using the random numbers 1 through 10, where 1, 2, 3, 4, 5, and 6 represent games in which she pitches. The player wants to simulate the 20 games that her team will play in the next month. Here are the results: 2, 5, 3, 9, 8, 6, 8, 4, 3, 1, 2, 9, 10, 5, 5, 7, 1, 6, 10, 4. In how many games does the simulation predict that the pitcher will appear?
    a. 7   b. 10   c. 13   d. 20

22. Find the median of this set of data: 12, 9, 14, 28, 17, 21, 25.
    a. 17   b. 18   c. 21   d. 28

23. Find the median of this set of data: 21, 16, 18, 24, 36, 28, 32, 41.
    a. 20   b. 26   c. 27   d. 41

24. Find the mean of this set of data: 15, 15, 18, 24, 31, 45, 48.
    a. 15   b. 24   c. 28   d. 33

25. Find the mean of this set of data: 16, 20, 20, 30, 40, 47, 87, 100.
    a. 84   b. 45   c. 35   d. 16

26. Find the range of this set of data: 21, 34, 56, 60, 10, 85, 76.
    a. 55   b. 64   c. 66   d. 75

27. Find the mode of this set of data: 12, 14, 15, 14, 20, 12, 21, 14, 12, 30, 14.
    a. 12   b. 14   c. 18   d. 30

28. The scatter plot shows the average number of points that a basketball team scored over the years from 1988 to 1996. How many points did the team average in 1994?
    a. 103   b. 104   c. 105   d. 106

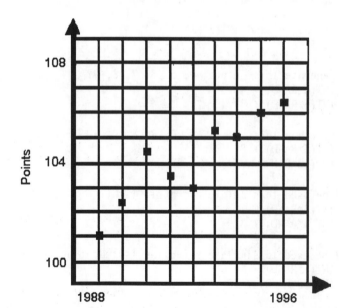

29. In the Venn diagram, set A is the set of students who own dogs, and set B is the set of students who own cats.

How many students shown in the Venn diagram own dogs?
a. 20   b. 13   c. 7   d. 6

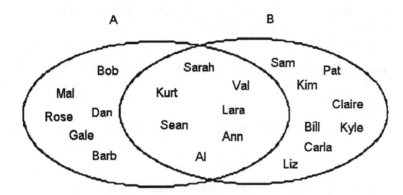

30. How many students shown in the Venn diagram own dogs AND cats?
a. 20   b. 14   c. 7   d. 0

31. This table shows the types of cars driven by the students in a class.

	Sports car	Compact	Mid-size	Van
Boys	3	6	5	1
Girls	3	7	3	2

How many students in the table are boys OR drive compact cars?
a. 30   b. 28   c. 22   d. 15

32. How many students in the table are girls AND drive vans?
a. 30   b. 16   c. 13   d. 2

33. The results of a survey on whether or not students in a class worked after school are shown in this table.

	Work	Don't work
Girls	11	4
Boys	12	5

How many students in the table are girls OR work after school?
a. 11   b. 15   c. 20   d. 27

34. How many students in the table are boys AND work after school?
a. 12   b. 23   c. 28   d. 32

35. A basketball team has 5 seniors, 4 juniors, 3 sophomores, and 1 freshman. The coach wants to appoint an older player as captain. In how many ways can the coach pick a senior OR a junior for captain?
a. 20   b. 13   c. 9   d. 0

36. A pizzeria has 5 meat toppings and 7·vegetable toppings. The pizzeria offers a special price on a pizza with 1 meat topping and 1 vegetable topping. In how many ways can a customer choose 1 meat topping AND 1 vegetable topping?
a. 2   b. 12   c. 20   d. 35

37. A bowling club has 15 right-handed members and 5 left-handed members. The club wants to send 1 right-handed member and 1 left-handed member to the state tournament. In how many ways can the club select 1 right-handed member AND 1 left-handed member to send?
a. 10   b. 20   c. 75   d. 125

38. Claire took 4 pairs of pants, 8 shirts, and 2 sweaters on vacation. In how many ways can Claire choose a pair of pants, a shirt, and a sweater to wear when going out to dinner?
   a. 14   b. 34   c. 64   d. 82

39. A restaurant has 5 entrees, 3 desserts, and 6 drinks on their lunch menu. The lunch special consists of 1 entree, 1 dessert, and 1 drink. In how many ways can a person select 1 entree, 1 dessert, and 1 drink from this restaurant's menu?
   a. 90   b. 21   c. 6   d. 1

40. How many ways are there to arrange the letters of the word *math*, using each letter exactly once?
   a. 4   b. 12   c. 16   d. 24

41. How many ways are there to arrange the letters of the word *phone*, using each letter exactly once?
   a. 200   b. 120   c. 60   d. 5

42. How many ways are there to arrange the letters of the word *computer*, using each letter exactly once?
   a. 8   b. 72   d. 620   d. 40,320

43. There are 9 boys and 11 girls in a class. If a person from the class is randomly selected, what is the probability that the person is a boy?
   a. $\frac{9}{2}$ b. $\frac{9}{11}$ c. $\frac{9}{20}$ d. $\frac{9}{99}$

44. A number cube is rolled once. What is the probability that the result is greater than or equal to 3?
   a. $\frac{2}{3}$ b. $\frac{1}{2}$ c. $\frac{1}{3}$ d. $\frac{1}{6}$

45. There are 5 red marbles, 4 green marbles, and 6 blue marbles in a bag. If a marble is randomly selected from the bag, what is the probability that the marble is green?
   a. $\frac{4}{30}$ b. $\frac{4}{15}$ c. $\frac{4}{11}$ d. $\frac{4}{6}$

46. If an integer between 1 and 15 inclusive is randomly selected, find the probability that the integer is a multiple of 6.
   a. $\frac{6}{15}$ b. $\frac{4}{15}$ c. $\frac{2}{15}$ d. $\frac{1}{15}$

47. If an integer between 1 and 21 inclusive is randomly selected, find the probability that the integer is a multiple of 6 OR a multiple of 8.
   a. $\frac{5}{21}$ b. $\frac{14}{21}$ c. $\frac{6}{8}$ d. $\frac{8}{6}$

48. This table shows the number of students taking math classes at Greenacres High School this year.

	Freshmen	Sophomores	Juniors	Seniors
Girls	20	18	17	15
Boys	23	17	15	15

If a math student at Greenacres High School this year is randomly selected, find the probability that the student is a boy OR a junior.
   a. $\frac{1}{2}$ b. $\frac{15}{140}$ c. $\frac{87}{140}$ d. $\frac{3}{4}$

49. If a math student at Greenacres High School this year is randomly selected, find the probability that the student is a girl AND a sophomore.

a. $\frac{3}{7}$
b. $\frac{87}{140}$
c. $\frac{1}{2}$
d. $\frac{18}{140}$

50. A fair coin is tossed, and heads comes up. What is the probability that heads comes up on the next toss of the coin?

a. 1
b. $\frac{1}{2}$
c. $\frac{1}{4}$
d. 0

51. A number cube is rolled, and the result is 2. What is the probability that the result is 2 on the next roll of the number cube?

a. 0
b. 1
c. $\frac{1}{5}$
d. $\frac{1}{6}$

52. A number cube is rolled twice. Find the probability that the result is an even number on both rolls.

a. $\frac{1}{4}$
b. $\frac{1}{3}$
c. $\frac{1}{6}$
d. $\frac{1}{12}$

53. A number cube is rolled twice. Find the probability that the result is 6 on both rolls.

a. $\frac{1}{3}$
b. $\frac{1}{6}$
c. $\frac{1}{12}$
d. $\frac{1}{36}$

54. Seven chips numbered 1, 2, 3, 4, 5, 6, and 7 are placed in a bag. A chip is randomly drawn and replaced. A second chip is then randomly drawn. Find the probability that both chips are even.

a. $\frac{3}{7}$
b. $\frac{9}{49}$
c. $\frac{6}{7}$
d. $\frac{6}{49}$

55. There are 5 red marbles, 3 green marbles, and 2 blue marbles in a bag. A marble is randomly selected and replaced. A second marble is then randomly selected. Find the probability that both marbles are green.

a. $\frac{3}{10}$
b. $\frac{3}{20}$
c. $\frac{9}{20}$
d. $\frac{9}{100}$

56. A standard deck of 52 cards includes 4 aces. A card is randomly selected from a standard deck of cards and replaced. A second card is then randomly selected from the deck. What is the probability that both cards are aces?

a. $\frac{4}{52} = \frac{1}{13}$
b. $\frac{16}{104} = \frac{2}{13}$
c. $\frac{16}{2704} = \frac{1}{169}$
d. $\frac{64}{2704} = \frac{4}{169}$

SHORT ANSWER. Write the answer in the space provided.

57. Find the theoretical probability that the spinner will land on an even number when spun.

_____

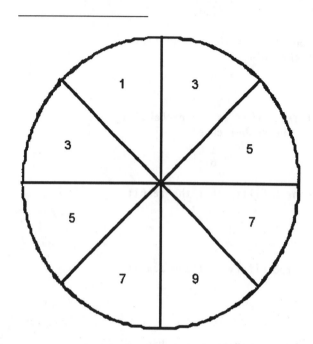

58. In practice, a basketball player shoots two free throws 20 times. The player records Y when the free throw is made and N when it is missed. Here are the results from one practice: YY, YY, YN, YN, YY, NN, NY, YY, YY, NY, NN, YY, YN, NN, NY, YY, YY, NY, YY, NY. What is the experimental probability in this case that the player misses both free throws?

_____

59. Sal tosses two coins 25 times with the following results: HT, TT, TH, HH, TH, TH, HH, HT, HH, HT, HT, TH, HT, HH, HT, TT, TH, HT, HH, HH, HT, TH, TT, TH, HH. What is the experimental probability in this case that one coin comes up heads and the other coin comes up tails?

_____

60. A player throws darts at a target that has 4 regions. The results are shown in this table.

Region	1	2	3	4
Frequency	10	7	5	3

Find the experimental probability that this player hits region 4 with a dart.

_____

61. A softball player keeps track of the number of hits she gets in a game. The results are shown in this table.

Hits	0	1	2	3	4	5
Frequency	4	9	8	5	3	1

Find the experimental probability that this player gets exactly 3 hits in her next game.

_____

62. Write the output of the command INT(5*RAND) + 3.

_____

63. Write the output of the command INT(3*RAND) + 10.

_____

64. Write a command to generate this output: 2, 3, 4, 5, 6, 7, 8, 9, 10.

_____

65. Write a command to generate this output: 6, 7, 8, 9.

_____

66. Write a command that could be used to simulate choosing 1 player out of 12 players.

_____

67. Write a command that could be used to simulate choosing 1 restaurant out of 20 restaurants.

_____

68. You must take a multiple-choice test. Each question has 4 possible answers. You do not know the answers to 15 of the questions and must guess on them. Describe a simulation to predict the number of correct answers you will guess on the 15 questions.

_____

_____

69. A traffic officer believes that 20% of the motorists that pass a point on the highway are speeding. If the officer is correct, describe a simulation to predict how many of the next 20 motorists that pass that point on the highway are speeding.

_____

_____

70. There are 2 red marbles, 4 blue marbles, and 7 green marbles in a bag. Describe a simulation to predict how many times a person will pick a blue marble from the bag in 10 trials.

_____

_____

71. Find the median and the range of this set of data: 58, 25, 28, 86, 41, 46, 91, 98, 200.

_____

72. Find the median and mode of this set of data: 6, 2, 75, 40, 79, 75, 60, 2, 24, 75.

_____

73. Five construction workers were paid the following amounts last week: $450, $920, $225, $365, and $395. Find the median and the mean amount that the five workers were paid.

_____

74. The table gives the number of customers at a store last week.

Day	Monday	Tuesday	Wednesday	Thursday	Friday	Saturday
Customers	132	145	112	152	245	468

Find the mean and mode number of customers per day at the store last week.

_____

75. Here are the number of points scored by the players on the basketball team in their last game: 6, 24, 12, 6, 10, 12, 6, 0, 2, 8. Find the mean and mode for the number of points scored.

_____

76. If the range of scores is 65, the median score is 102, and the highest score is 150, find the lowest score.

_____

77. The following table shows the average speed at a car race from 1992 to 1996.

Year	1992	1993	1994	1995	1996
Average speed(mph)	124.5	131	132.5	128	133.2

Make a scatter plot of the data.

78. In a class of 30 students, 14 are on the basketball team, and 9 are on the track team. This includes 4 who are on both teams. Show this in a Venn diagram. Include all 30 students.

79. Forty families in a neighborhood own dogs OR cats. Twenty-five families own dogs, and 30 families own cats. How many families own dogs AND cats?

_____

80. List the integers from 1 to 20 inclusive that are multiples of 4 OR multiples of 3.

_____

81. The table shows what type of centers are in a gift box of chocolates.

	Coconut	Caramel	Peanut
Dark chocolate	5	4	3
Milk chocolate	3	8	2

How many dark chocolate candies are in the box represented by the table? How many of the chocolates are dark chocolates OR have caramel centers?

_____

82. How many milk chocolate candies are in the box? How many of the chocolates are milk chocolates AND have coconut centers?

_____

83. This table shows the results of a survey on what students do most
    after school on weekdays.

	Homework	Job	Watch TV
Boys	20	14	5
Girls	22	16	6

How many of the students in the survey spend most of their time doing
homework? How many students in the survey are girls AND spend most of
their time doing homework?

_____

84. How many of the students in the survey spend most of their time at their jobs? How many
    students in the survey are boys OR spend most of their time at their jobs?

_____

85. There are four blood groups: O, A, B, and AB. Each blood group can have two Rh types:
    positive and negative. Make a tree diagram to show all the different possible blood
    types.

86. Two people decide to have 2 children. Make a tree diagram to show all the possible ways
    of having 2 children.

87. A pet store has 12 birds, 8 dogs, 5 cats, and 9 hamsters for sale. A person can't decide
    whether to buy a dog or a hamster, so the person decides to buy both. In how many ways
    can the person choose 1 dog AND 1 hamster?

_____

88. A clothing store carries jackets in 3 styles. Each style comes in 8 colors and 4 sizes.
    How many jackets must the store carry in order to have one jacket of each combination?

_____

89. A drama club has 5 male members and 6 female members. The club decides to put on a play
    with a cast that includes a male lead, a female lead, and a supporting role that can be
    played by either a male or female. In how many ways can the club choose the male lead AND
    the female lead? In how many ways can the club choose the entire cast of the play?

_____

90. How many ways are there to arrange the letters of the word *basket*, using each letter
    exactly once?

_____

91. The manager of a fast-food restaurant has 5 employees. The manager needs a person to take
    orders, a person to fry hamburgers, a person to make french fries, a person to bag
    orders, and a person to clean. The manager moves the workers around so that they don't
    always do the same job. In how many ways can the manager assign the 5 workers to a job?

_____

92. There were 20 adult tickets, 15 student tickets, and 10 child tickets sold to a concert.
    If one of the ticket holders is randomly selected for a door prize, find the probability
    that the ticket holder is a student.

_____

93. Jan owns 15 rock CDs, 8 country CDs, and 5 rap CDs. If Jan randomly selects one of her CDs, find the probability that it is a rock CD.

_____

94. If an integer between 1 and 25 inclusive is randomly selected, find the probability that the integer is a multiple of 7.

_____

95. If an integer between 1 and 24 inclusive is randomly selected, find the probability that the integer is a multiple of 5 OR a multiple of 9.

_____

96. If an integer between 1 and 30 inclusive is randomly selected, find the probability that the integer is a multiple of 3 AND a multiple of 4.

_____

97. A company asks its employees which television network's news they watch. The results are shown in this table.

	ABC	NBC	CBS	FOX
Women	12	15	8	5
Men	10	9	17	4

If one of this company's employees is randomly selected, find the probability that the person is a woman OR watches NBC news.

_____

98. If one of this company's employees is randomly selected, find the probability that the person is a man AND watches CBS news.

_____

99. A standard deck of 52 cards contains 4 kings. A card is randomly selected from a standard deck and then replaced. A second card is then randomly selected from the deck. If the first card selected is a king, what is the probability that the second card is also a king? Are the two selections from the deck independent events? Explain.

_____

_____

100. A standard deck of 52 cards contains 4 queens. A card is randomly selected from a standard deck and not replaced. A second card is then randomly selected from the deck. If the first card selected is a queen, what is the probability that the second card is also a queen? Are the two selections from the deck independent events? Explain.

_____

_____

101. A number cube is rolled, and the result is 1. Find the probability that the result on the next roll of the number cube is less than 3.

_____

102. A number cube is rolled twice. Find the probability that the result on both rolls is less than 3.

_____

103. Seven chips numbered 1, 2, 3, 4, 5, 6, and 7 are placed in a bag. A chip is randomly drawn and replaced. A second chip is then randomly drawn. Find the probability that both chips are odd.

_____

104. There are 5 red marbles, 3 green marbles, and 2 blue marbles in a bag. A marble is randomly selected and replaced. A second marble is then randomly selected. Find the probability that both marbles are blue.

_____

105. A standard deck of cards contains 13 hearts. A card is randomly selected from a standard deck of cards and replaced. A second card is then randomly selected from the deck. Find the probability that at least 1 of the cards is a heart.

_____

ANSWERS TO CHAPTER 4

1. Answer: b Section: 1 Objective: 1a

2. Answer: a Section: 2 Objective: 2a

3. Answer: b Section: 3 Objective: 3a

4. Answer: b Section: 4 Objective: 4b

5. Answer: b Section: 5 Objective: 5b

6. Answer: a Section: 6 Objective: 6a

7. Answer: c Section: 7 Objective: 7a

8. Answer:
   d. $\frac{1}{8}$

   Section: 1 Objective: 1a

9. Answer:
   c. $\frac{1}{6}$

   Section: 1 Objective: 1b

10. Answer:
    d. $\frac{4}{15}$

    Section: 1 Objective: 1b

11. Answer:
    b. $\frac{9}{20}$

    Section: 1 Objective: 1b

12. Answer:
    a. $\frac{7}{25}$

    Section: 1 Objective: 1b

13. Answer: d. 2, 3, 4, 5 Section: 1 Objective: 1b

14. Answer: c. 4, 5, 6 Section: 1 Objective: 1b

15. Answer: b. INT(6*RAND) + 4 Section: 2 Objective: 2a

16. Answer: c. INT(8*RAND) + 5 Section: 2 Objective: 2a

17. Answer: b. INT(3*RAND) Section: 2 Objective: 2a

18. Answer: c. INT(30*RAND) + 1 Section: 2 Objective: 2a

19. Answer: d. INT(5*RAND) Section: 2 Objective: 2a

20. Answer: c. 5 Section: 2 Objective: 2a

21. Answer: c. 13 Section: 2 Objective: 2a

22. Answer: a. 17 Section: 3 Objective: 3a

23. Answer: b. 26 Section: 3 Objective: 3a

24. Answer: c. 28 Section: 3 Objective: 3a

25. Answer: b. 45 Section: 3 Objective: 3a

26. Answer: d. 75 Section: 3 Objective: 3a

27. Answer: b. 14 Section: 3 Objective: 3a

28. Answer: c. 105 Section: 3 Objective: 3b

29. Answer: b. 13 Section: 4 Objective: 4a

30. Answer: c. 7 Section: 4 Objective: 4a

31. Answer: c. 22 Section: 4 Objective: 4b

32. Answer: d. 2 Section: 4 Objective: 4b

33. Answer: d. 27 Section: 4 Objective: 4b

34. Answer: a. 12 Section: 4 Objective: 4b

35. Answer: c. 9 Section: 4 Objective: 4b

36. Answer: d. 35 Section: 5 Objective: 5b

37. Answer: c. 75 Section: 5 Objective: 5b

38. Answer: c. 64 Section: 5 Objective: 5b

39. Answer: a. 90 Section: 5 Objective: 5b

40. Answer: d. 24 Section: 5 Objective: 5b

41. Answer: b. 120 Section: 5 Objective: 5b

42. Answer: d. 40,320 Section: 5 Objective: 5b

43. Answer:
    c. $\frac{9}{20}$

    Section: 6 Objective: 6a

44. Answer:
    a. $\frac{2}{3}$

    Section: 6 Objective: 6a

45. Answer:
    b. $\frac{4}{15}$

    Section: 6 Objective: 6a

46. Answer:
    c. $\frac{2}{15}$

    Section: 6 Objective: 6a

47. Answer:
    a. $\frac{5}{21}$

    Section: 6 Objective: 6b

48. Answer:
    c. $\frac{87}{140}$

    Section: 6 Objective: 6b

49. Answer:
    d. $\frac{18}{140}$

    Section: 6 Objective: 6b

50. Answer:
    b. $\frac{1}{2}$

    Section: 7 Objective: 7a

51. Answer:
    d. $\frac{1}{6}$

    Section: 7 Objective: 7a

52. Answer:
a. $\frac{1}{4}$

Section: 7 Objective: 7b

53. Answer:
d. $\frac{1}{36}$

Section: 7 Objective: 7b

54. Answer:
b. $\frac{9}{49}$

Section: 7 Objective: 7b

55. Answer:
d. $\frac{9}{100}$

Section: 7 Objective: 7b

56. Answer:
c. $\frac{16}{2704} = \frac{1}{169}$

Section: 7 Objective: 7b

57. Answer: 0 Section: 1 Objective: 1a

58. Answer:
$\frac{3}{20}$

Section: 1 Objective: 1b

59. Answer:
$\frac{15}{25} = \frac{3}{5}$

Section: 1 Objective: 1b

60. Answer:
$\frac{3}{25}$

Section: 1 Objective: 1b

61. Answer:
$\frac{5}{30} = \frac{1}{6}$

Section: 1 Objective: 1b

62. Answer: 3, 4, 5, 6, 7   Section: 1   Objective: 1b

63. Answer: 10, 11, 12   Section: 1   Objective: 1b

64. Answer: INT(9*RAND) + 2   Section: 2   Objective: 2a

65. Answer: INT(4*RAND) + 6   Section: 2   Objective: 2a

66. Answer: Answers may vary. Sample: INT(12*RAND) + n Section: 2   Objective: 2a

67. Answer: Answers may vary. Sample: INT(20*RAND) + n Section: 2   Objective: 2a

68. Answer:
Answers will vary. Use INT(4*RAND) to generate the random integers 0 through 3. Assign 0 to a correct guess. Generate 15 random integers and count the number of times that 0 occurs.

Section: 2   Objective: 2a

69. Answer:
Answers will vary. Use INT(10*RAND) to generate the random integers 0 through 9. Assign 0 and 1 to be speeders. Generate 20 random integers and count the number of times 0 and 1 occur.

Section: 2   Objective: 2a

70. Answer:
Answers will vary. Use INT(13*RAND) to generate the random integers 0 through 12. Assign 0, 1, 2, and 3 to be blue marbles. Generate 10 random integers and count the number of times 0, 1, 2, and 3 occur.

Section: 2   Objective: 2a

71. Answer: median = 58; range = 175   Section: 3   Objective: 3a

72. Answer: median = 50; mode = 75   Section: 3   Objective: 3a

73. Answer: median = $395; mean = $471   Section: 3   Objective: 3a

74. Answer: mean = 209 customers; no mode   Section: 3   Objective: 3a

75. Answer: mean = 8.6; mode = 6   Section: 3   Objective: 3a

76. Answer: 85   Section: 3   Objective: 3a

77. Answer:

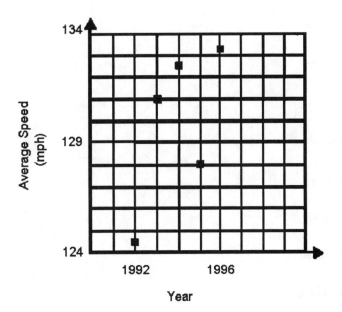

Section: 3 Objective: 3b

78. Answer:

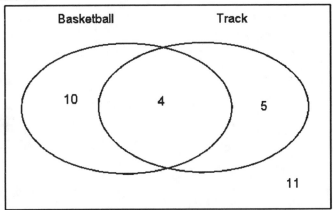

Section: 4 Objective: 4a

79. Answer: 15 families Section: 4 Objective: 4b

80. Answer: 3, 4, 6, 8, 9, 12, 15, 16, 18, 20 Section: 4 Objective: 4b

81. Answer: 12; 20 Section: 4 Objective: 4b

82. Answer: 13; 3 Section: 4 Objective: 4b

83. Answer: 42; 22 Section: 4 Objective: 4b

84. Answer: 30; 55 Section: 4 Objective: 4b

85. Answer:

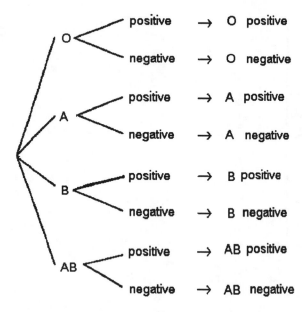

Section: 5 Objective: 5a

86. Answer:

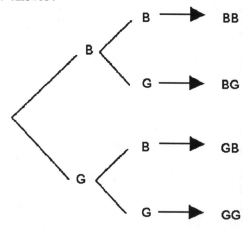

Section: 5 Objective: 5a

87. Answer: 72 Section: 5 Objective: 5b

88. Answer: 96 jackets Section: 5 Objective: 5b

89. Answer: 30; 270 Section: 5 Objective: 5b

90. Answer: 720 Section: 5 Objective: 5b

91. Answer: 120 Section: 5 Objective: 5b

92. Answer:
$$\frac{15}{45} = \frac{1}{3}$$

Section: 6 Objective: 6a

93. Answer:

$\frac{15}{28}$

Section: 6 Objective: 6a

94. Answer:

$\frac{3}{25}$

Section: 6 Objective: 6a

95. Answer:

$\frac{6}{24} = \frac{1}{4}$

Section: 6 Objective: 6b

96. Answer:

$\frac{2}{30} = \frac{1}{15}$

Section: 6 Objective: 6b

97. Answer:

$\frac{49}{80}$

Section: 6 Objective: 6b

98. Answer:

$\frac{17}{80}$

Section: 6 Objective: 6b

99. Answer:

$\frac{4}{52} = \frac{1}{13}$; yes. Since the first card is replaced, the probability of getting a king on the second selection is not affected by what happened on the first selection. The deck does not remember what happened on the first selection.

Section: 7 Objective: 7a

100. Answer:

$\frac{3}{51}$, no. Since the first queen is not replaced, there are fewer cards and fewer queens available for the second selection, so the probability of selecting a queen on the second selection is affected by what happened on the first selection.

Section: 7 Objective: 7a

101. Answer:
$$\frac{2}{6} = \frac{1}{3}$$

Section: 7   Objective: 7a

102. Answer:
$$\frac{4}{36} = \frac{1}{9}$$

Section: 7   Objective: 7b

103. Answer:
$$\frac{16}{49}$$

Section: 7   Objective: 7b

104. Answer:
$$\frac{4}{100} = \frac{1}{25}$$

Section: 7   Objective: 7b

105. Answer:
$$1 - \frac{9}{16} = \frac{7}{16}$$

Section: 7   Objective: 7b

CHAPTER 5: *Transformations*

QUANTITATIVE COMPARISON

In the space provided, write:
a. if the quantity in Column A is greater than the quantity in Column B;
b. if the quantity in Column B is greater than the quantity in Column A;
c. if the two quantities are equal; or
d. if the relationship cannot be determined from the information given.

Column A	Column B	Answer

1.

$f(3)$ when $f(x) = x^2$	$f(3)$ when $f(x) = 2^x$	_____

2.

The y-coordinate of the lowest point on the graph of $y = |x + 3|$	The y-coordinate of the lowest point on the graph of $y = |x| + 3$	_____

3.

The scale factor of the function $y = 3x^2$	The scale factor of the function $y = \dfrac{x^2}{4}$	_____

4.

The maximum y-coordinate of the function $y = -|x|$	The minimum y-coordinate of the function $y = x^2$	_____

5.

The point (2, 3) is on the graph of a function. The x-coordinate of the point after a horizontal translation of 7 is applied to the graph	The point (2, 3) is on the graph of a function. The y-coordinate of the point after a vertical translation of 7 is applied to the graph	_____

6. The point (5, 2) is on the graph of a function. The graph is given a horizontal translation of 6 followed by a vertical stretch by a factor of 5.

The x-coordinate of the point after the transformations are applied	The y-coordinate of the point after the transformations are applied	_____

MULTIPLE CHOICE. Circle the letter of the best answer choice.

7. Which of the following sets of ordered pairs is a function?
   a. $\{(3, 0), (5, 3), (3, 5)\}$ b. $\{(4, 6), (6, 4), (8, 2)\}$
   c. $\{(3, 6), (3, 9), (3, 12)\}$ d. $\{(9, 6), (-9, 7), (9, 9)\}$

8. Which of the following sets of ordered pairs is a function?
   a. $\{(8, 2), (8, 3), (8, 4)\}$ b. $\{(1, 6), (-1, 4), (1, 2)\}$
   c. $\{(5, 6), (3, 9), (1, 6)\}$ d. $\{(7, 6), (7, -6), (6, -7)\}$

9. What is the domain of this function: $\{(2, 6), (4, 9), (6, 12), (8, 15)\}$?
   a. $\{2, 4, 6, 8, 9, 12, 15\}$ b. $\{2, 4, 6, 8\}$
   c. $\{6, 9, 12, 15\}$ d. $\{8, 13, 18, 23\}$

10. What is the range of this function: $\{(1, 2), (2, 4), (3, 8), (4, 16)\}$?
    a. $\{2, 4\}$ b. $\{1, 2, 3, 4, 8, 16\}$
    c. $\{1, 2, 3, 4\}$ d. $\{2, 4, 8, 16\}$

11. Find $f(2)$ if $f(x) = 3^x$.
    a. 6   b. 8   c. 9   d. 32

12. Find $g(-4)$ if $g(x) = x^2$.
    a. -8   b. 16   c. -16   d. 42

13. Find $h(-4)$ if $h(x) = |x - 5|$.
    a. -1   b. -9   c. 1   d. 9

14. Which of the following is the parent function of the function graphed here?

    a. $y = x$ b. $y = \dfrac{1}{x}$ c. $y = |x|$ d. $y = x^2$

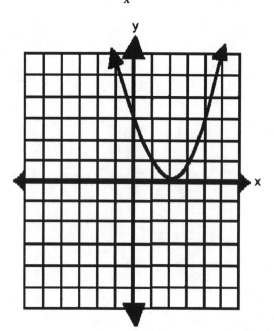

15. Which of the following is the parent function of the function graphed here?

    a. $y = x$ 　　 b. $y = \dfrac{1}{x}$ 　　 c. $y = |x|$ 　　 d. $y = x^2$

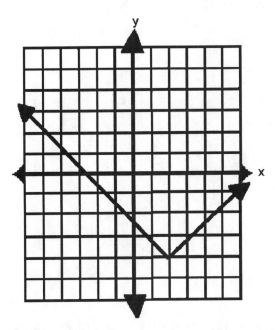

16. Which of the following transformations is applied to the graph of $y = |x|$ when $y = 2|x|$ is graphed?

    a. stretch 　　 b. reflection 　　 c. shift 　　 d. all of these

17. Which of the following transformations is applied to the graph of $y = \dfrac{1}{x}$ when $y = \dfrac{1}{x-2}$ is graphed?

    a. stretch 　　 b. reflection 　　 c. shift 　　 d. all of these

18. Which of the following transformations is applied to the graph of $y = |x|$ to get the graph shown?

    a. stretch 　　 b. reflection 　　 c. shift 　　 d. all of these

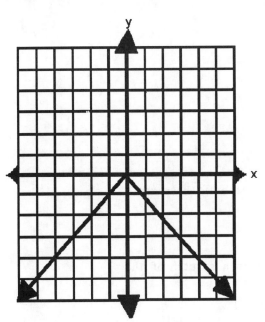

19. Which of the following transformations is applied to the graph of $y = x^2$ to get the graph shown?

a. stretch   b. reflection   c. shift   d. all of these

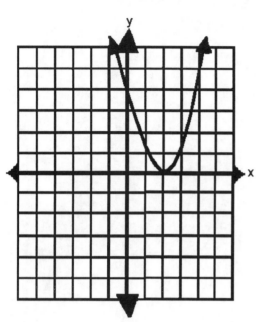

20. Which of the following transformations is applied to the graph of $y = |x|$ to get the graph shown?

a. stretch   b. reflection   c. shift   d. all of these

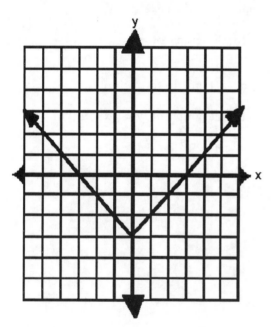

21. Which of the following functions results in a stretch of the parent function?

a. $y = -x^2$ b. $y = \dfrac{3}{x}$ c. $y = x - 6$ d. $y = |2 + x|$

22. Which of the following functions does not result in a stretch of the parent function?

a. $y = \dfrac{x^2}{5}$ b. $y = \dfrac{7}{x}$ c. $y = 2x$ d. $y = (x + 2)^2$

90

23. Which of the following functions results in the greatest stretch of the graph of $y = x^2$?

     a. $y = \frac{1}{2}x^2$ b. $y = \frac{2}{3}x^2$ c. $y = \frac{1}{4}x^2$ d. $y = \frac{2}{5}x^2$

24. Identify the scale factor of the function $y = \frac{9}{x}$.

     a. 9   b. -9   c. $\frac{1}{9}$ d. $\frac{-1}{9}$

25. Identify the scale factor of the function $y = \frac{x^2}{6}$.

     a. 6   b. -6   c. $\frac{1}{6}$ d. $\frac{-1}{6}$

26. Which of the following is the equation of the function graphed?

     a. $y = |x|$ b. $y = |x + 3|$ c. $y = 3|x|$ d. $y = \frac{|x|}{3}$

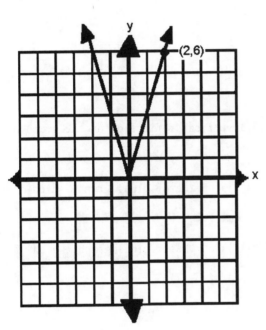

27. Which of the following is the equation of the function graphed?

   a. $y = x$ b. $y = x^2 + 2$ c. $y = 2x^2$ d. $y = \dfrac{x^2}{2}$

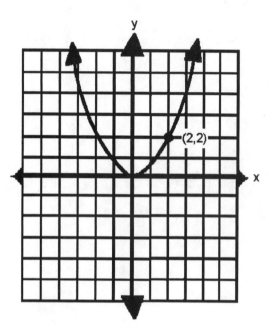

28. The graph of which of the following functions is a vertical reflection of the graph of $y = x^2$?

   a. $y = 3x^2$ b. $y = x^2 - 1$ c. $y = -x^2$ d. $y = (-x)^2$

29. A graph is reflected through the x-axis. If (2, 8) is on the original graph, which of the following points is on the reflected graph?

   a. (8, 2)   b. (-2, 8)   c. (2, -8)   d. (-2, -8)

30. A graph is reflected through the y-axis. If (5, 7) is on the original graph, which of the following points is on the reflected graph?

   a. (-5, -7)   b. (7, 5)   c. (5, -7)   d. (-5, 7)

31. Which of the following functions will have the minimum point (0, 0)?

   a. $y = -3x^2$ b. $y = -|x|$ c. $y = \dfrac{x^2}{-2}$ d. $y = |4x|$

32. Which of the following functions will have the maximum point (0, 0)?

   a. $y = x^2 - 2$ b. $y = |x - 1|$ c. $y = \dfrac{-x^2}{3}$ d. $y = \dfrac{|x|}{6}$

33. Which of the following functions will have the minimum point (0, 0)?

   a. $y = -x^2$ b. $y = |-x|$ c. $y = \dfrac{x^2}{-1}$ d. $y = -|x|$

34. The point (6, 9) is on the graph of a function. Which of the following points is on the graph after a vertical translation of 8?

   a. (14, 9)   b. (14, 17)   c. (6, 17)   d. (6, 1)

35. The point (9, 12) is on the graph of a function. Which of the following points is on the graph after a horizontal translation of 8?

   a. (9, 4)   b. (17, 20)   c. (9, 20)   d. (17, 12)

36. The graph of which of the following functions is a translation of the graph of the parent function?

a. $y = 3x^2$ b. $y = \dfrac{1}{x-3}$ c. $y = -5|x|$ d. $y = \dfrac{x}{3}$

37. Which translation of the graph of the parent function $y = x^2$ gives the graph of the function $y = x^2 + 3$?

a. vertical translation of 3

b. vertical translation of -3

c. horizontal translation of 3

d. horizontal translation of -3

38. Which translation of the graph of the parent function $y = x^2$ gives the graph of the function $y = (x + 5)^2$?

a. vertical translation of 5

b. vertical translation of -5

c. horizontal translation of 5

d. horizontal translation of -5

39. Which of the following is the equation of the translation shown of the graph of the parent function $y = |x|$?

a. $y = |x| - 3$ b. $y = |x| + 3$ c. $y = |x - 3|$ d. $y = |x + 3|$

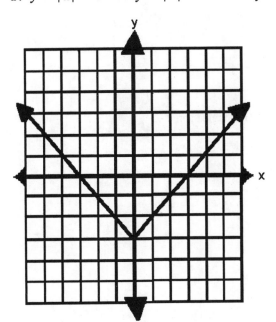

40. Which of the following is the equation of the translation shown of the graph of the parent function $y = |x|$?
   a. $y = |x| - 5$ b. $y = |x| + 5$ c. $y = |x - 5|$ d. $y = |x + 5|$

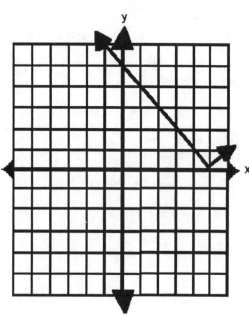

41. Which of the following is the parent function of the function graphed?
   a. $y = \dfrac{1}{x}$ b. $y = 2^x$ c. $y = x^2$ d. $y = |x|$

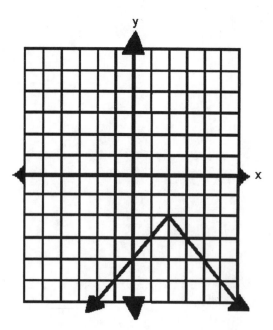

42. Which of the following are the coordinates of the point (5, 8) after a vertical translation of 7 followed by a horizontal translation of -5?
   a. (15, 0)   b. (12, 3)   c. (0, 15)   d. (10, 15)

43. Which of the following are the coordinates of the point (2, 3) after a vertical stretch of 4 followed by a vertical translation of 6?
   a. (8, 18)   b. (14, 12)   c. (2, 36)   d. (2, 18)

44. Which of the following are the coordinates of the point (1, 4) after a horizontal translation of 5 followed by a vertical reflection?
    a. (-6, 4)   b. (6, -4)   c. (1, -9)   d. (-1, 9)

45. Which of the following functions is graphed here?
    a. $y = |x + 3| + 1$
    b. $y = |x + 1| + 3$
    c. $y = |x - 3| + 1$
    d. $y = |x - 1| + 3$

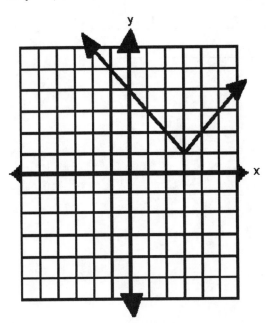

46. Which of the following functions is graphed here?
    a. $y = -x^2 + 2$ b. $y = -x^2 - 2$ c. $y = -(x + 2)^2$ d. $y = -(x - 2)^2$

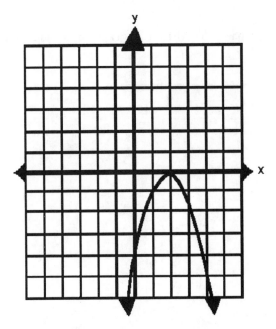

SHORT ANSWER. Write the answer in the space provided.

47. State the domain and range of this set of ordered pairs: {(2, 6), (5, 9), (8, 12), (11, 9)}. Is the set a function?

48. State the domain and range of this set of ordered pairs: {(5, 8), (10, 12), (5, 16), (10, 20)}. Is the set a function?

_____

49. Find the domain and range of the set of points graphed. Is this the graph of a function? Explain.

_____

_____

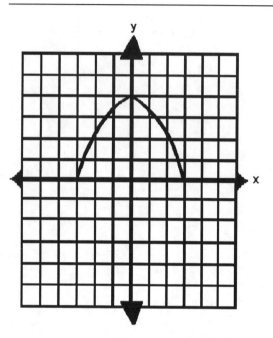

50. Find the domain and range of the set of points graphed. Is this the graph of a function? Explain.

_____

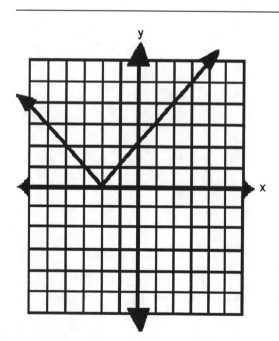

51. Find $f(3)$ if $f(x) = 5^x$.

    _____

52. Find $f(-8)$ if $f(x) = |x + 3|$.

    _____

53. Find $f(8)$ if $f(x) = x^2 - 3$.

    _____

54. Graph $y = 2 + |x|$. Tell whether the graph of $y = |x|$ is stretched, reflected, or shifted.

    _____

55. Graph $2|x|$. Tell whether the graph of $y = |x|$ is stretched, reflected, or shifted.

    _____

56. Name the parent function of the function graphed here. What transformation was applied to the graph of the parent function?

    _____

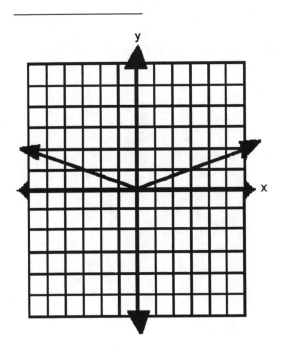

57. Name the parent function of the function graphed here. What transformation was applied to the graph of the parent function?

_____

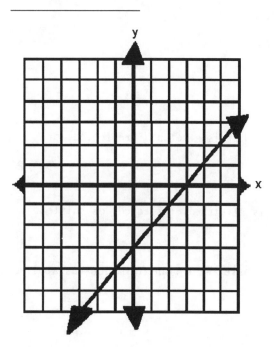

58. Name the parent function of the function graphed here. What transformation was applied to the graph of the parent function?

_____

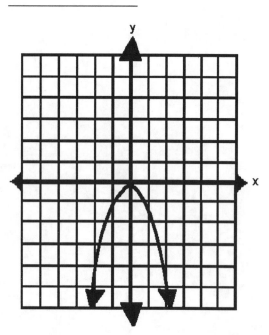

59. Graph $y = \frac{1}{4}x^2$. Describe how the parent function was changed by the $\frac{1}{4}$.

_____

60. What happens to the point (1, 5) on a parent function when the parent function is stretched vertically by a factor of 3?

_____

61. Identify the scale factor of the function $y = 8x^2$.

_____

62. Identify the scale factor of the function $y = \dfrac{1}{5x}$.

_____

63. Write an equation for the function graphed.

_____

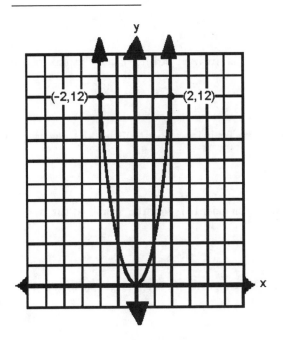

64. Write an equation for the function graphed.

_____

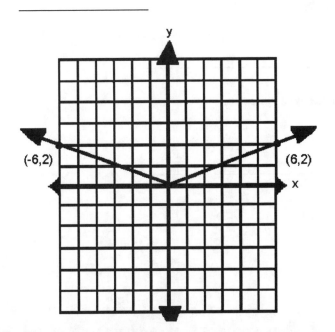

65. Write the equation of the graph that is a vertical reflection of the graph of $y = x^2$.

   _____

66. Write the equation of the graph that is a horizontal reflection of the graph of $y = 4x + 2$.

   _____

67. A graph is reflected through the x-axis. If (6, 3) is on the original graph, which point is on the reflected graph?

   _____

68. A graph is reflected through the y-axis. If (7, 5) is on the original graph, which point is on the reflected graph?

   _____

69. Graph $y = -3^x$.

70. Will the graph of $y = (-x)^2$ have a maximum point or a minimum point? Find the maximum or minimum point.

   _____

71. Will the graph of $y = -5|x|$ have a maximum point or a minimum point? Find the maximum or minimum point.

   _____

72. The point (2, 9) is on the graph of a function. Which point is on the graph after a horizontal translation of 6?

   _____

73. The point (4, 15) is on the graph of a function. Which point is on the graph after a vertical translation of 12?

   _____

74. Which translation of the graph of the parent function $y = \dfrac{1}{x}$ gives the

   graph of the function $y = \dfrac{1}{x} - 7$?

   _____

75. Which translation of the graph of the parent function $y = \dfrac{1}{x}$ gives the

   graph of the function $y = \dfrac{1}{x - 6}$?

   _____

76. The graph shown is a translation of the graph of the parent function $y = x^2$. Write the equation of the graph.

_____

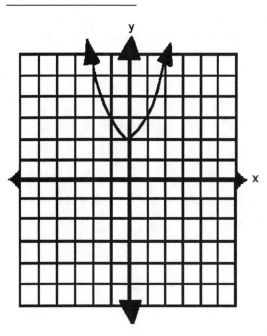

77. The graph shown is a translation of the graph of the parent function $y = x^2$. Write the equation of the graph.

_____

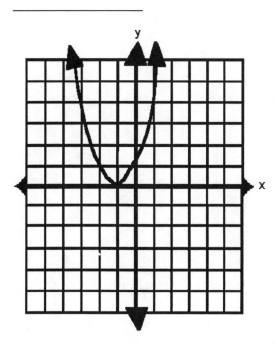

78. Graph $y = |x - 3|$. What translation is applied to the graph of the parent function?

_____

79. What is the parent function of $y = 2(x + 3)^2 - 5$?

_____

80. What is the parent function of $y = \dfrac{7}{x + 3} + 5$?

_____

81. What are the coordinates of the point (2, 4) after a horizontal translation of -8 followed by a vertical translation of 5?

_____

82. What are the coordinates of the point (-3, 5) after a vertical stretch by a factor of 6 followed by a vertical translation of 6?

_____

83. What are the coordinates of the point (7, 8) after a horizontal reflection followed by a horizontal translation of -5?

_____

84. Graph $y = (x - 2)^2 + 1$.

85. Graph $y = -|x + 2|$.

ANSWERS TO CHAPTER 5

1. Answer: a   Section: 1   Objective: 1c

2. Answer: b   Section: 2   Objective: 2a

3. Answer: a   Section: 3   Objective: 3b

4. Answer: c   Section: 4   Objective: 4b

5. Answer: b   Section: 5   Objective: 5a

6. Answer: a   Section: 6   Objective: 6b

7. Answer: b. $\{(4, 6), (6, 4), (8, 2)\}$ Section: 1   Objective: 1a

8. Answer: c. $\{(5, 6), (3, 9), (1, 6)\}$ Section: 1   Objective: 1a

9. Answer: b. $\{2, 4, 6, 8\}$ Section: 1   Objective: 1a

10. Answer: d. $\{2, 4, 8, 16\}$ Section: 1   Objective: 1a

11. Answer: c. 9   Section: 1   Objective: 1c

12. Answer: b. 16   Section: 1   Objective: 1c

13. Answer: d. 9   Section: 1   Objective: 1c

14. Answer: d. $y = x^2$ Section: 2   Objective: 2a

15. Answer: c. $y = |x|$ Section: 2   Objective: 2a

16. Answer: a. stretch   Section: 2   Objective: 2a

17. Answer: c. shift   Section: 2   Objective: 2a

18. Answer: b. reflection   Section: 2   Objective: 2b

19. Answer: c. shift   Section: 2   Objective: 2b

20. Answer: c. shift   Section: 2   Objective: 2b

21. Answer:
    b. $y = \dfrac{3}{x}$

    Section: 3   Objective: 3a

22. Answer: d. $y = (x + 2)^2$ Section: 3   Objective: 3a

23. Answer:
    b. $y = \dfrac{2}{3}x^2$

    Section: 3   Objective: 3a

24. Answer: a. 9 Section: 3 Objective: 3b

25. Answer:
    c. $\dfrac{1}{6}$

    Section: 3 Objective: 3b

26. Answer: c. $y = 3|x|$ Section: 3 Objective: 3b

27. Answer:
    d. $y = \dfrac{x^2}{2}$

    Section: 3 Objective: 3b

28. Answer: c. $y = -x^2$ Section: 4 Objective: 4a

29. Answer: c. $(2, -8)$ Section: 4 Objective: 4a

30. Answer: d. $(-5, 7)$ Section: 4 Objective: 4a

31. Answer: d. $y = |4x|$ Section: 4 Objective: 4b

32. Answer:
    c. $y = \dfrac{-x^2}{3}$

    Section: 4 Objective: 4b

33. Answer: b. $y = |-x|$ Section: 4 Objective: 4b

34. Answer: c. $(6, 17)$ Section: 5 Objective: 5a

35. Answer: d. $(17, 12)$ Section: 5 Objective: 5a

36. Answer:
    b. $y = \dfrac{1}{x - 3}$

    Section: 5 Objective: 5a

37. Answer: a. vertical translation of 3 Section: 5 Objective: 5b

38. Answer: d. horizontal translation of -5 Section: 5 Objective: 5b

39. Answer: a. $y = |x| - 3$ Section: 5 Objective: 5b

40. Answer: c. $y = |x - 5|$ Section: 5 Objective: 5b

41. Answer: d. $y = |x|$ Section: 6 Objective: 6a

42. Answer: c. $(0, 15)$ Section: 6 Objective: 6b

43. Answer: d. (2, 18)   Section: 6   Objective: 6b

44. Answer: b. (6, -4)   Section: 6   Objective: 6b

45. Answer: c. $y = |x - 3| + 1$ Section: 6   Objective: 6b

46. Answer: d. $y = -(x - 2)^2$ Section: 6   Objective: 6b

47. Answer: domain: {2, 5, 8, 11}; range: {6, 9, 12}; yes   Section: 1   Objective: 1a

48. Answer: domain: {5, 10}; range: {8, 12, 16, 20}; no   Section: 1   Objective: 1a

49. Answer:
    Domain: $-3 \leq x \leq 3$; range: $0 \leq y \leq 4$. Yes; any vertical line that intersects the graph
    will intersect it exactly once.

    Section: 1   Objective: 1b

50. Answer:
    Domain: all numbers; range: $y \geq 0$. Yes; any vertical line will intersect the graph
    exactly once.

    Section: 1   Objective: 1b

51. Answer: $f(3) = 125$ Section: 1   Objective: 1c

52. Answer: $f(-8) = 5$ Section: 1   Objective: 1c

53. Answer: $f(8) = 61$ Section: 1   Objective: 1c

54. Answer: shifted

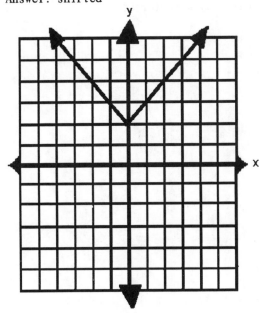

    Section: 2   Objective: 2a

55. Answer: stretched

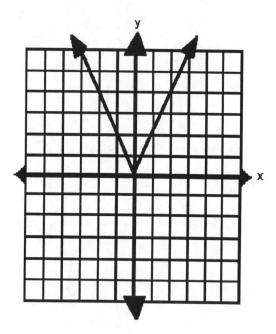

Section: 2 Objective: 2a

56. Answer: $y = |x|$; stretch Section: 2 Objective: 2b

57. Answer: $y = x$; shift Section: 2 Objective: 2b

58. Answer: $y = x^2$; reflection Section: 2 Objective: 2b

59. Answer:
    Each point on the parent graph is stretched vertically by a factor of
    $\frac{1}{4}$.

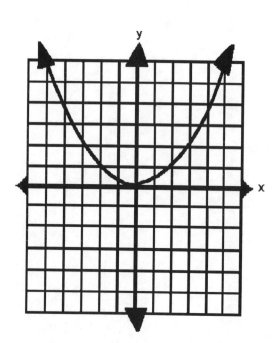

60. Answer: The point $(1, 5)$ becomes the point $(1, 15)$ on the transformed graph. Section: 3
    Objective: 3a

61. Answer: 8 Section: 3 Objective: 3b

62. Answer:
    $\dfrac{1}{5}$
    Section: 3 Objective: 3b

63. Answer: $y = 3x^2$ Section: 3 Objective: 3b

64. Answer:
    $y = \dfrac{|x|}{3}$ or $y = \left|\dfrac{x}{3}\right|$
    Section: 3 Objective: 3b

65. Answer: $y = -x^2$ Section: 4 Objective: 4a

66. Answer: $y = 4(-x) + 2$ or $y = -4x + 2$ Section: 4 Objective: 4a

67. Answer: $(6, -3)$ Section: 4 Objective: 4a

68. Answer: $(-7, 5)$ Section: 4 Objective: 4a

69. Answer:

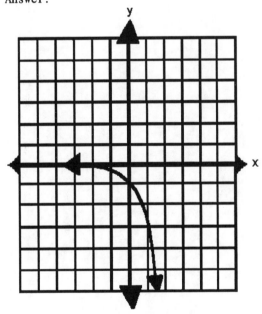

    Section: 4 Objective: 4a

70. Answer: minimum point at $(0, 0)$ Section: 4 Objective: 4b

71. Answer: maximum point at (0, 0) Section: 4 Objective: 4b

72. Answer: (8, 9) Section: 5 Objective: 5a

73. Answer: (4, 27) Section: 5 Objective: 5a

74. Answer: vertical translation of -7 Section: 5 Objective: 5b

75. Answer: horizontal translation of 6 Section: 5 Objective: 5b

76. Answer: $y = x^2 + 2$ Section: 5 Objective: 5b

77. Answer: $y = (x + 1)^2$ Section: 5 Objective: 5b

78. Answer: horizontal translation of 3

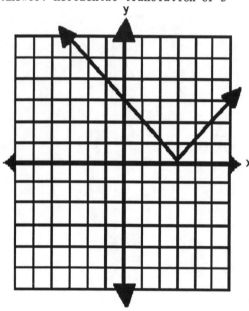

Section: 5 Objective: 5b

79. Answer: $y = x^2$ Section: 6 Objective: 6a

80. Answer:
$y = \dfrac{1}{x}$

Section: 6 Objective: 6a

81. Answer: (-6, 9) Section: 6 Objective: 6b

82. Answer: (-3, 36) Section: 6 Objective: 6b

83. Answer: (-12, 8) Section: 6 Objective: 6b

84. Answer:

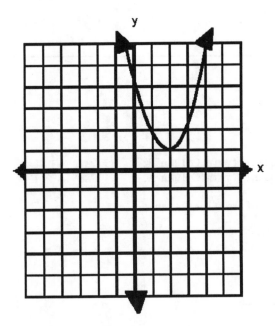

Section: 6 Objective: 6b

85. Answer:

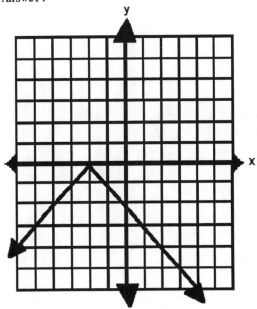

Section: 6 Objective: 6b

CHAPTER 6: Exponents

QUANTITATIVE COMPARISON

In the space provided, write:
a. if the quantity in Column A is greater than the quantity in Column B;
b. if the quantity in Column B is greater than the quantity in Column A;
c. if the two quantities are equal; or
d. if the relationship cannot be determined from the information given.

Column A	Column B	Answer

1.

| $2^3 \cdot 2^4$ | $2^6 \cdot 2^2$ | _____ |

2.

| $(2^2)^4$ | $(2^3)^3$ | _____ |

3.

| 12^0 | 6^0 | _____ |

4.

| 6×10^{18} | 6,000,000,000,000,000 | _____ |

5.   The population of Argos is 2000 and is growing at a rate of 3% a year. The population of Mentone is 2300 and is growing at a rate of 2% a year.

| The population of Argos in 10 years if the growth rate stays the same | The population of Mentone in 10 years if the growth rate rate stays the same | _____ |

6.   The population of Akron is 5000 and is increasing at a rate of 4% a year. The population of Rochester is 12,000 and is decreasing at a rate of 5% a year.

| The population of Akron in 10 years if the rate of increase stays the same | The population of Rochester in 10 years if the rate of decrease stays the same | _____ |

MULTIPLE CHOICE. Circle the letter of the best answer choice.

7. Which of the following is another expression for 16?
   a. 1^{16} b. 4^4 c. 2^4 d. 8^2

8. Which of the following is another expression for 12?
   a. 12^1 b. 4^3 c. 2^6 d. 1^{12}

9. Simplify: $5^3 \cdot 5^5$.
   a. 5^2 b. 5^8 c. 5^{15} d. 5^{243}

10. Simplify: $\dfrac{3^8}{3^2}$.
    a. 3^{16} b. 3^{10} c. 3^6 d. 3^4

11. Simplify: $2^3 + 2^5$.
    a. 32,768   b. 256   c. 40   d. 4

12. Simplify: $x^6 \cdot x^4 \cdot x^2$.
    a. x^{48} b. x^{36} c. x^{24} d. x^{12}

13. Simplify: $\dfrac{y^{10} \cdot y^6}{y^4}$.
    a. y^{15} b. y^{12} c. y^4 d. y^2

14. Which of the following is a monomial?
    a. $3x^2 + 6$ b. $(2x)(3x)$ c. $4(x + 3)$ d. $7 - x$

15. Which of the following is not a monomial?
    a. 6   b. $7x^3 y^4$ c. $(3x^2)(5y)$ d. $x - 4$

16. Simplify: $(5x^3)(8x^5)$.
    a. $13x^8$ b. $40x^{15}$ c. $13x^{15}$ d. $40x^8$

17. Simplify: $(-3x^4 y^2)(-5x^3 y^5)$.
    a. $-8x^7 y^7$ b. $15x^7 y^7$ c. $-15x^{12} y^{10}$ d. $8x^{12} y^{10}$

18. Simplify: $(2x^4)^3$.
    a. $2x^7$ b. $2x^{12}$ c. $8x^7$ d. $8x^{12}$

19. Simplify: $\dfrac{12y^{10}}{6y^2}$.
    a. $2y^8$ b. $6y^5$ c. $2y^5$ d. $6y^8$

20. Simplify: $\dfrac{x^6 y^{12}}{x^3 y^4}$.
    a. $x^2 y^3$ b. $x^2 y^8$ c. $x^3 y^8$ d. $x^3 y^3$

21. Simplify: $(2x)^0$.
    a. $2x$ b. x c. 2   d. 1

22. Simplify: 3^{-2}.
    a. 9   b. –6   c. $\dfrac{1}{9}$ d. $\dfrac{-1}{6}$

23. Write $x^3 y^{-4}$ without negative or zero exponents.
    a. $-x^3 y^4$ b. $\dfrac{1}{x^3 y^4}$ c. $\dfrac{-x^3}{y^4}$ d. $\dfrac{x^3}{y^4}$

24. Write $x^{-8} x^5$ without negative or zero exponents.
    a. $\dfrac{1}{x^3}$ b. $\dfrac{1}{x^{13}}$ c. $\dfrac{1}{x^{40}}$ d. $\dfrac{1}{x^{150}}$

25. Write $(2y^{-3})(5y^{-5})$ without negative or zero exponents.
    a. $-10y^{15}$ b. $10y^{15}$ c. $\dfrac{-10}{y^8}$ d. $\dfrac{10}{y^8}$

26. Write $\dfrac{x^3}{x^{-5}}$ without negative or zero exponents.

   a. x^8 b. x^2 c. $\dfrac{1}{x^2}$ d. $\dfrac{1}{x^8}$

27. Write $\dfrac{x^{-8}}{x^{-2}}$ without negative or zero exponents.

   a. x^4 b. $\dfrac{1}{x^4}$ c. $\dfrac{1}{x^6}$ d. $\dfrac{1}{x^{10}}$

28. Write 0.000000000065 in scientific notation.
   a. 6.5×10^{11} b. 6.5×10^{10} c. 6.5×10^{-11} d. 6.5×10^{-10}

29. Write 2.5×10^{-4} in customary notation.
   a. 250,000   b. 25,000   c. 0.0025   d. 0.00025

30. Find the product: $(2 \times 10^5)(4 \times 10^7)$.
   a. 8×10^{35} b. 6×10^{12} c. 8×10^{12} d. 6×10^{35}

31. Find the product: $(5 \times 10^6)(6 \times 10^8)$.
   a. 3,000,000,000,000,000   b. 300,000,000,000,000
   c. 30,000,000,000,000,000   d. 30,000,000,000,000

32. Find the quotient: $\dfrac{9 \times 10^{12}}{3 \times 10^3}$.
   a. 3×10^4 b. 6×10^4 c. 3×10^9 d. 6×10^9

33. Find the quotient: $\dfrac{8 \times 10^6}{5 \times 10^4}$.
   a. 1600   b. 160   c. 16   d. 1.6

34. Simplify: $\dfrac{(9 \times 10^6)(4 \times 10^4)}{6 \times 10^5}$.
   a. 6×10^5 b. 6×10^4 c. 6×10^2 d. 6×10^1

35. The population of Marshall is growing at a rate of 2.5% a year. What multiplier is used to predict the new population each year?
   a. 2.5   b. 1.25   c. 1.025   d. 1.0025

36. The population of Brown County is growing at a rate of 0.7% a year. What multiplier is used to predict the new population each year?
   a. 1.7   b. 1.07   c. 1.007   d. 7

37. The population of Greenfield is 10,000 and is growing at a rate of 4% a year. Predict the population of Greenfield in 5 years if the growth rate stays the same.
   a. 53,782   b. 40,000   c. 24,673   d. 12,167

38. The population of Deerfield is 20,000 and is growing at a rate of 0.7% a year. Predict the population of Deerfield in 8 years if the growth rate stays the same.
   a. 171,200   b. 34,364   c. 21,148   d. 20,112

39. Which of the following is an exponential function?

   a. $y = x^2$ b. $y = 1.5^x$ c. $y = \dfrac{x}{6}$ d. $y = x^5$

40. Which of the following functions is graphed here?
   a. $y = 3^x$ b. $y = 1.3^x$ c. $y = 0.3^x$ d. $y = x^3$

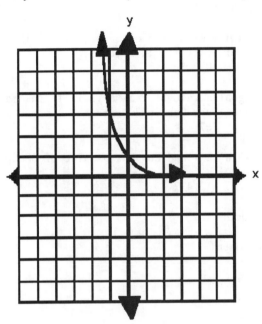

41. Which of the following functions is graphed here?
   a. $y = 2^x$ b. $y = 2^x + 2$ c. $y = 0.2^x$ d. $y = 0.2^x + 2$

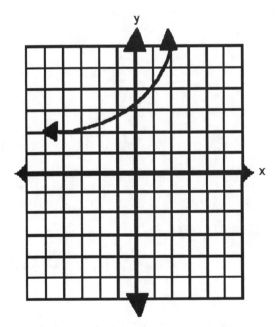

42. The value of an investment is decreasing at a rate of 7% a year. What multiplier is used to predict the new value of the investment each year?
   a. 0.93 b. 1.07 c: -0.93 d. -1.07

43. The value of an investment has been growing at a rate of 7.5% a year and is now $3000. If the rate of growth stays the same, predict the value of the investment in 12 years.
   a. $7145 b. $5700 c. $4654 d. $3281

44. An investment has been growing at a rate of 6% a year and now has a value of $500. What was the value of the investment 4 years ago?
   a. $631 b. $452 c. $396 d. $380

45. An investment has been growing at a rate of 9% a year and now has a value of $1500. What was the value of the investment 7 years ago?
   a. $2742   b. $820   c. $735   d. $555

46. The population of Westville is 12,000 and is decreasing at a rate of 3% a year. If the rate of decrease stays the same, predict the population of Westville in 5 years.
   a. 13,911   b. 10,200   c. 13,800   d. 10,305

47. The population of Burr Oak is 900 and is decreasing at a rate of 1.5% a year. If the rate of decrease stays the same, predict the population of Burr Oak in 7 years.
   a. 999   b. 810   c. 799   d. 767

48. An investment has been losing money at a rate of 4% a year and now has a value of $8000. What was the value of the investment 4 years ago?
   a. $6795   b. $9419   c. $9280   d. $10,432

SHORT ANSWER. Write the answer in the space provided.

49. Express $x \cdot x \cdot x \cdot x \cdot x \cdot x \cdot x \cdot x$ with an exponent.

   _____

50. Evaluate: $3^3 + 3^4$.

   _____

51. Simplify: $7^2 \cdot 7^3$.

   _____

52. Simplify: $\dfrac{3^{16}}{3^4}$.

   _____

53. Simplify: $3^3 \cdot 3^2 \cdot 3^4$.

   _____

54. Simplify: $x^8 \cdot x^6$.

   _____

55. Simplify: $\dfrac{y^4 \cdot y^6}{y^2}$.

   _____

56. Find the product: $(5y^4)(4y^7)$. Is the product a monomial?

   _____

57. Simplify: $(3x^4)^2$. Is the result a monomial?

58. Find the product: $(-8x^5y^4)(7x^7y^3)$.

   _____

114

59. Simplify: $(2x^4 y^5)^3$.

_____

60. Simplify: $(x^3 y^5)^4 (x^2 y^3)^2$.

_____

61. Simplify: $\dfrac{-16x^{15}}{2x^5}$.

_____

62. Simplify: $\dfrac{9x^9 y^{16}}{3x^3 y^8}$.

_____

63. Write $(7x^3 y)^0$ without negative or zero exponents.

_____

64. Write $5x^{-3}$ without negative or zero exponents.

_____

65. Simplify: $y^6 y^{-8}$. Write your answer without negative or zero exponents.

_____

66. Simplify: $x^{-5} x^{-7}$. Write your answer without negative or zero exponents.

_____

67. Simplify: $(6x^{-4} y^5)(4x^8 y^{-7})$. Write your answer without negative or zero exponents.

_____

68. Simplify: $\dfrac{x^4}{x^{-5}}$. Write your answer without negative or zero exponents.

_____

69. Simplify: $\dfrac{x^{-8}}{x^{-4}}$. Write your answer without negative or zero exponents.

_____

70. Write 0.00000000000075 in scientific notation.

_____

71. Write 8.2×10^{-7} in customary notation.

_____

72. Find the product: $(2 \times 10^5)(3 \times 10^9)$. Write your answer in customary notation.

_____

73. Find the product: $(8 \times 10^4)(9 \times 10^3)$. Write your answer in customary notation.

   _____

74. Find the quotient: $\dfrac{8 \times 10^{14}}{2 \times 10^4}$. Write your answer in scientific notation.

   _____

75. Find the quotient: $\dfrac{3 \times 10^{10}}{5 \times 10^6}$. Write your answer in scientific notation.

   _____

76. Simplify: $\dfrac{(6 \times 10^5)(8 \times 10^3)}{4 \times 10^4}$. Write your answer in scientific notation.

   _____

77. The population of Green County is growing at a rate of 3.7% a year. What multiplier is used to predict the new population each year?

   _____

78. The population of Red River is growing at a rate of 0.9% a year. What multiplier is used to predict the new population each year?

   _____

79. The population of Salem is 15,000 and is growing at a rate of 2.7% a year. Write a function to model the population of Salem. If the rate of growth stays the same, predict the population of Salem in 6 years.

   _____

80. The population of Cold Springs is 45,000 and is growing at a rate of 0.5% a year. Write a function to model the population of Cold Springs. If the rate of growth stays the same, predict the population of Cold Springs in 7 years.

   _____

81. The population of Wellville is 120,000 and is growing at a rate of 0.65% a year. Write a function to model the population of Wellville. If the rate of growth stays the same, predict the population of Wellville in 10 years.

   _____

82. Graph $y = 3^x$.

83. Graph $y = 0.2^x$.

84. The population of a city is decreasing at a rate of 9% a year. What multiplier is used to predict the new population of the city each year?

   _____

85. The value of an investment has been growing at a rate of 4.5% a year and is now $6000. Write a function to model the value of the investment. If the rate of growth stays the same, predict the value of the investment in 10 years.

_____

86. An investment has been growing at a rate of 8% a year and now has a value of $900. Write a function to model the value of the investment. What was the value of the investment 6 years ago?

_____

87. An investment has been growing at a rate of 5.8% a year and now has a value of $15,000. Write a function to model the value of the investment. What was the value of the investment 8 years ago?

_____

88. The population of Cool Harbor is 6700 and is decreasing at a rate of 8% a year. Write a function to model the population of Cool Harbor. If the rate of decrease stays the same, predict the population of Cool Harbor in 4 years.

_____

89. The population of Ora is 16,000 and is decreasing at a rate of 3.5% a year. Write a function to model the population of Ora. If the rate of decrease stays the same, predict the population of Ora in 15 years.

_____

90. An investment has been losing money at a rate of 7% a year and now has a value of $6500. Write a function to model the value of the investment. What was the value of the investment 5 years ago?

_____

1. Answer: b Section: 1 Objective: 1b

2. Answer: b Section: 2 Objective: 2b

3. Answer: c Section: 3 Objective: 3a

4. Answer: a Section: 4 Objective: 4a

5. Answer: b Section: 5 Objective: 5a

6. Answer: a Section: 6 Objective: 6b

7. Answer: c. 2^4 Section: 1 Objective: 1a

8. Answer: a. 12^1 Section: 1 Objective: 1a

9. Answer: b. 5^8 Section: 1 Objective: 1b

10. Answer: c. 3^6 Section: 1 Objective: 1b

11. Answer: c. 40 Section: 1 Objective: 1b

12. Answer: d. x^{12} Section: 1 Objective: 1b

13. Answer: b. y^{12} Section: 1 Objective: 1b

14. Answer: b. $(2x)(3x)$ Section: 2 Objective: 2a

15. Answer: d. $x - 4$ Section: 2 Objective: 2a

16. Answer: d. $40x^8$ Section: 2 Objective: 2b

17. Answer: b. $15x^7y^7$ Section: 2 Objective: 2b

18. Answer: d. $8x^{12}$ Section: 2 Objective: 2b

19. Answer: a. $2y^8$ Section: 2 Objective: 2b

20. Answer: c. x^3y^8 Section: 2 Objective: 2b

21. Answer: d. 1 Section: 3 Objective: 3a

22. Answer:
    c. $\dfrac{1}{9}$

    Section: 3 Objective: 3a

23. Answer:
    d. $\dfrac{x^3}{y^4}$

    Section: 3 Objective: 3a

24. Answer:

a. $\dfrac{1}{x^3}$

Section: 3 Objective: 3b

25. Answer:

d. $\dfrac{10}{y^8}$

Section: 3 Objective: 3b

26. Answer: a. x^8 Section: 3 Objective: 3b

27. Answer:

c. $\dfrac{1}{x^6}$

Section: 3 Objective: 3b

28. Answer: c. 6.5×10^{-11} Section: 4 Objective: 4a

29. Answer: d. 0.00025 Section: 4 Objective: 4a

30. Answer: c. 8×10^{12} Section: 4 Objective: 4b

31. Answer: a. 3,000,000,000,000,000 Section: 4 Objective: 4b

32. Answer: c. 3×10^9 Section: 4 Objective: 4b

33. Answer: b. 160 Section: 4 Objective: 4b

34. Answer: a. 6×10^5 Section: 4 Objective: 4b

35. Answer: c. 1.025 Section: 5 Objective: 5a

36. Answer: c. 1.007 Section: 5 Objective: 5a

37. Answer: d. 12,167 Section: 5 Objective: 5a

38. Answer: c. 21,148 Section: 5 Objective: 5a

39. Answer: b. $y = 1.5^x$ Section: 5 Objective: 5a

40. Answer: c. $y = 0.3^x$ Section: 5 Objective: 5b

41. Answer: b. $y = 2^x + 2$ Section: 5 Objective: 5b

42. Answer: a. 0.93 Section: 6 Objective: 6a

43. Answer: a. $7145 Section: 6 Objective: 6a

44. Answer: c. $396 Section: 6 Objective: 6a

45. Answer: b. $820 Section: 6 Objective: 6a

46. Answer: d. 10,305   Section: 6   Objective: 6b

47. Answer: b. 810   Section: 6   Objective: 6b

48. Answer: b. $9419   Section: 6   Objective: 6b

49. Answer: x^8 Section: 1   Objective: 1a

50. Answer: 108   Section: 1   Objective: 1a

51. Answer: $7^5 = 16,807$ Section: 1   Objective: 1b

52. Answer: $3^{12} = 531,441$ Section: 1   Objective: 1b

53. Answer: $3^9 = 19,683$ Section: 1   Objective: 1b

54. Answer: x^{14} Section: 1   Objective: 1b

55. Answer: y^8 Section: 1   Objective: 1b

56. Answer: $20y^{11}$; yes   Section: 2   Objective: 2a

57. Answer:
$9x^8$; yes

Section: 2   Objective: 2a

58. Answer: $-56x^{12}y^7$ Section: 2   Objective: 2b

59. Answer: $8x^{12}y^{15}$ Section: 2   Objective: 2b

60. Answer: $x^{16}y^{26}$ Section: 2   Objective: 2b

61. Answer: $-8x^{10}$ Section: 2   Objective: 2b

62. Answer: $3x^6y^8$ Section: 2   Objective: 2b

63. Answer: 1   Section: 3   Objective: 3a

64. Answer:
$\dfrac{5}{x^3}$

Section: 3   Objective: 3a

65. Answer:
$\dfrac{1}{y^2}$

Section: 3   Objective: 3b

66. Answer:
$\dfrac{1}{x^{12}}$

Section: 3   Objective: 3b

67. Answer:
$$\frac{24x^4}{y^2}$$
Section: 3 Objective: 3b

68. Answer: x^9 Section: 3 Objective: 3b

69. Answer:
$$\frac{1}{x^4}$$
Section: 3 Objective: 3b

70. Answer: 7.5×10^{-13} Section: 4 Objective: 4a

71. Answer: 0.00000082 Section: 4 Objective: 4a

72. Answer: 600,000,000,000,000 Section: 4 Objective: 4b

73. Answer: 720,000,000 Section: 4 Objective: 4b

74. Answer: 4×10^{10} Section: 4 Objective: 4b

75. Answer: 6×10^3 Section: 4 Objective: 4b

76. Answer: 1.2×10^5 Section: 4 Objective: 4b

77. Answer: 1.037 Section: 5 Objective: 5a

78. Answer: 1.009 Section: 5 Objective: 5a

79. Answer: $P = 15,000(1.027)^x$; about 17,600 Section: 5 Objective: 5a

80. Answer: $P = 45,000(1.005)^x$; about 46,600 Section: 5 Objective: 5a

81. Answer: $P = 120,000(1.0065)^x$; about 128,000 Section: 5 Objective: 5a

82. Answer:

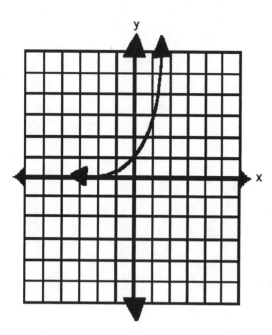

Section: 5   Objective: 5b

83. Answer:

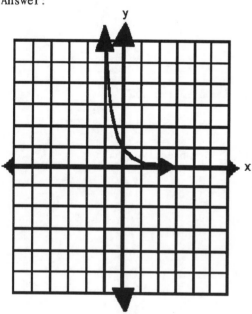

Section: 5   Objective: 5b

84. Answer: 0.91   Section: 6   Objective: 6a

85. Answer: $y = 6000(1.045)^x$; about \$9318   Section: 6   Objective: 6a

86. Answer: $y = 900(1.08)^x$; about \$567   Section: 6   Objective: 6a

87. Answer: $y = 15,000(1.058)^x$; about $9554 Section: 6 Objective: 6a

88. Answer: $y = 6700(0.92)^x$; about 4800 Section: 6 Objective: 6b

89. Answer: $y = 16,000(0.965)^x$; about 9376 Section: 6 Objective: 6b

90. Answer: $y = 6500(0.93)^x$; about $9343 Section: 6 Objective: 6b

CHAPTER 7: Polynomials and Factoring

QUANTITATIVE COMPARISON

In the space provided, write:
a. if the quantity in Column A is greater than the quantity in Column B;
b. if the quantity in Column B is greater than the quantity in Column A;
c. if the two quantities are equal; or
d. if the relationship cannot be determined from the information given.

Column A	Column B	Answer

1.

The value of $x^2 + 2x - 35$ when $x = 6$	The value of $(x - 5)(x + 7)$ when $x = 6$

_____

2.

$2x^2 + 3x - 9$ $+ (3x^2 + 4x + 9)$	$8x^2 + 5x - 9$ $- (3x^2 - 2x - 9)$

_____

3. For a given value of x

$x(x - 1)$	$x(x + 1)$

_____

4. For a given value of x

$(x + 2)(x - 2)$	$(x + 3)(x - 3)$

_____

5.

The GCF of $12x^2$ and 15	The GCF of $12x$ and 8

_____

6.

The missing term in this perfect-square trinomial $x^2 + 8x +$ ___	The missing term in this perfect-square trinomial $x^2 - 10x +$ ___

_____

7.

The number of ways $x^2 - 8x + 12$ can be factored by using binomials	The number of ways $x^2 - x + 12$ can be factored by using binomials

_____

MULTIPLE CHOICE. Circle the letter of the best answer choice.

8. Find the value of $x^2 + 5x + 15$ when $x = 8$.
   a. 71   b. 109   c. 119   d. 143

9. Find the value of $x^2 + 3x - 30$ when $x = -5$.
   a. -70   b. -20   c. 10   d. 40

10. Find the value of $(x + 6)(x - 9)$ when $x = 7$.
    a. 208   b. 26   c. -208   d. -26

11. Find the value of $(x - 3)(x + 4)$ when $x = -8$.
    a. 44   b. 20   c. -44   d. -20

12. The surface area of a hemisphere with a radius of r is given by the function $S(r) = 3\pi r^2$. Find the surface area of a hemisphere with a radius of 5 inches.
    a. 47.1 in.^{2} b. 235.6 in.^{2} c. 876.4 in.^{2} d. 2220.6 in.^{2}

13. The volume of a sphere with a radius of r is given by the function
    $V(r) = \dfrac{4\pi r^3}{3}$. Find the volume of a sphere with a radius of 3 feet.
    a. 12.6 ft^3 b. 37.7 ft^3 c. 113.1 ft^3 d. 339.3 ft^3

14. The surface area of a container with a radius of r is given by the function $S(r) = 2\pi r^2 + 10\pi r$ with r in centimeters. Find the surface area of a container with a radius of 4 cm.
    a. 100.5 cm^2 b. 140.5 cm^2 c. 150.8 cm^2 d. 226.2 cm^2

15. Which of the following polynomials has degree 3?
    a. $3x + 3$ b. $x^2 + 3x + 3$ c. $x^3 - 1$ d. $x^4 + 3x^2 - 2x + 3$

16. Which of the following polynomials is a trinomial with degree 2?
    a. $x^3 - 3x + 1$ b. $3x^2 - 5x + 3$ c. $2x^3 - 2$ d. $4x^2 + 3x$

17. Add: $(3x^2 + 5x - 7) + (6x^2 - 2x + 10)$.
    a. $9x^2 + 7x + 17$ b. $9x^2 + 3x + 17$ c. $9x^2 - 3x + 3$ d. $9x^2 + 3x + 3$

18. Add: $(5x^3 + 2x + 5) + (6x^2 - 7x + 3)$.
    a. $11x^2 - 5x + 8$ b. $11x^2 + 5x + 8$
    c. $5x^3 + 6x^2 - 5x + 8$ d. $5x^3 + 6x^2 + 5x + 8$

19. Subtract: $(8x^2 + 5x - 2) - (3x^2 - 2x + 5)$.
    a. $5x^2 + 3x - 7$ b. $5x^2 + 7x - 7$ c. $5x^2 - 3x - 7$ d. $5x^2 + 7x + 3$

20. Subtract: $(4x^3 + 5x^2 + 9) - (2x^2 - 8x + 3)$.
    a. $2x^2 + 13x + 6$ b. $2x^2 - 3x + 6$
    c. $4x^3 + 3x^2 - 8x + 6$ d. $4x^3 + 3x^2 + 8x + 6$

21. Simplify: $7x + 5x^2 - 2 - (9 - 8x - 2x^2)$.
    a. $3x^2 + 15x - 11$ b. $7x^2 + 15x - 11$ c. $7x^2 - x - 11$ d. $3x^2 - 15x - 7$

22. Find the product: $7(x - 3)$.
    a. $7x - 3$ b. $x - 21$ c. $7x + 21$ d. $7x - 21$

23. Find the product: $-3(5x + 4)$.
    a. $-15x - 12$ b. $-15x + 4$ c. $-15x + 1$ d. $-15x - 7$

24. Find the product: $x(5 - 2x)$.
    a. $5 - 2x^2$ b. $5x - 2x^2$ c. $5x + 2x^2$ d. $3x$

25. Find two factors and a product for this model.
   a. $(x + 3)(x + 1) = x^2 + 2x + 3$ b. $(x - 3)(x - 1) = x^2 - 4x + 3$
   c. $(x + 3)(x - 1) = x^2 - 3x - 3$ d. $(x + 3)(x - 1) = x^2 + 2x - 3$

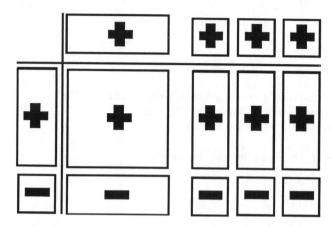

26. Find two factors and a product for this model.
   a. $(x - 2)(x - 3) = x^2 - x + 6$ b. $(x - 2)(x - 3) = x^2 - 5x + 6$
   c. $(x + 2)(x - 3) = x^2 - 5x - 6$ d. $(x - 2)(x - 3) = x^2 + 5x + 6$

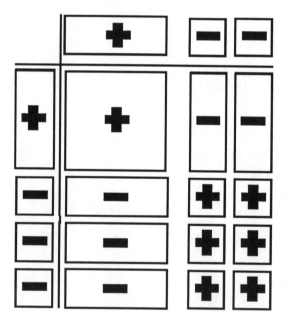

27. Find two factors and a product for this model.
    a. $(2x + 1)(2x - 2) = 4x^2 - 2x - 2$ b. $(2x + 1)(x - 2) = x^2 - 4x - 2$
    c. $(2x + 1)(x - 2) = 2x^2 - 3x - 2$ d. $(x + 1)(2x - 2) = x^2 + 3x - 2$

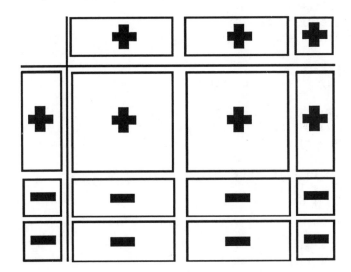

28. Find two factors and a product for this model.
    a. $(x - 3)(x - 1) = x^2 - 5x + 3$ b. $(2x + 3)(x - 1) = 2x^2 - 5x - 3$
    c. $(2x - 3)(x - 1) = 2x^2 + 5x + 3$ d. $(2x - 3)(x - 1) = 2x^2 - 5x + 3$

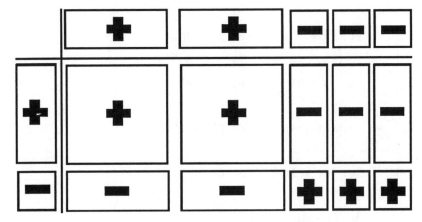

29. Use the Distributive Property to find the product: $(x + 5)(x + 6)$.
    a. $x^2 + 30x + 11$ b. $x^2 + 30x + 30$ c. $x^2 + 11x + 11$ d. $x^2 + 11x + 30$

30. Use the Distributive Property to find the product: $(x + 7)(x - 3)$.
    a. $x^2 + 4x + 21$ b. $x^2 + 4x - 21$ c. $x^2 - 4x + 21$ d. $x^2 - 4x - 21$

31. Use the Distributive Property to find the product: $(x - 5)(x - 8)$.
    a. $x^2 + 13x - 13$ b. $x^2 - 13x + 13$ c. $x^2 - 13x + 40$ d. $x^2 - 13x - 40$

32. Use the FOIL method to find the product: $(x - 6)(x + 2)$.
    a. $x^2 - 4x - 12$ b. $x^2 - 4x + 12$ c. $x^2 + 4x - 12$ d. $x^2 + 4x + 12$

33. Use the FOIL method to find the product: $(2x - 1)(x + 7)$.
    a. $2x^2 + 6x - 7$ b. $2x^2 - 6x - 7$ c. $2x^2 + 13x - 7$ d. $x^2 + 13x + 7$

34. Use the FOIL method to find the product: $(2x - 3)(3x - 1)$.
    a. $6x^2 - 4x + 3$ b. $5x^2 - 11x + 3$ c. $6x^2 - 11x - 3$ d. $6x^2 - 11x + 3$

35. Use the FOIL method to find the product: $(x + 3y)(x + 2y)$.
    a. $x^2 + 5xy + 6y^2$ b. $x^2 + 5xy + 5y^2$ c. $x^2 + 5y + 6y^2$ d. $x^2 + 5x + 6y^2$

36. Factor by removing the GCF: $12x^2 - 18x$.
    a. $6(2x^2 - 3x)$ b. $x(12x - 18)$ c. $6x(2x - 3)$ d. $6x^2(2 - 3x)$

37. Factor by removing the GCF: $4x^4 - 8x^3 + 6x^2$.
    a. $4x^2(x^2 - 4x + 2)$ b. $2x^2(2x^2 - 4x + 3)$
    c. $2(2x^4 - 4x^2 + 3x)$ d. $2x(2x^3 - 4x^2 + 3x)$

38. Factor by removing the GCF: $5x^3y + 10xy^2$.
    a. $5(x^3y + 2xy^2)$ b. $xy(5x^2 + 10y)$ c. $5xy(x^2 + y)$ d. $5xy(x^2 + 2y)$

39. Write as the product of two binomials: $4(x + 2) - x(x + 2)$.
    a. $(4 - x)(x + 2)$ b. $(4 + x)(x + 2)$
    c. $(x - 4)(x + 2)$ d. $(4 - x)(x - 2)$

40. Write as the product of two binomials: $3x(x - 5) + 6(x - 5)$.
    a. $(x + 6)(x - 5)$ b. $(3x + 1)(x - 5)$
    c. $(3x - 6)(x - 5)$ d. $(3x + 6)(x - 5)$

41. Factor: $5x + 5y + mx + my$.
    a. $5(x + y)(m + n)$ b. $(5 + m)(x + y)$
    c. $(5 + x)(m + y)$ d. $(5 + y)(m + x)$

42. Factor: $6ab + 4a + 15b + 10$.
    a. $(a + 6)(b + 5)$ b. $(2a + 4)(b + 5)$
    c. $(2a + 5)(3b + 2)$ d. $(5a + 2)(3b + 5)$

43. Factor: $x^2 + 20x + 100$.
    a. $(x + 10)^2$ b. $(x - 10)^2$ c. $(x + 50)^2$ d. $(x - 50)^2$

44. Factor: $x^2 - 12x + 36$.
    a. $(x + 18)^2$ b. $(x - 18)^2$ c. $(x + 6)^2$ d. $(x - 6)^2$

45. Factor: $9x^2 - 24x + 16$.
    a. $(3x - 8)^2$ b. $(3x + 8)^2$ c. $(3x - 4)^2$ d. $(3x + 4)^2$

46. Factor: $4x^2 + 20xy + 25y^2$.
    a. $(x + 5y)^2$ b. $(2x + 5y)^2$ c. $(4x + 5y)^2$ d. $(4x + 5)^2$

47. Factor: $x^2 - 64$.
    a. $(x - 32)(x + 32)$ b. $(x - 16)(x + 4)$
    c. $(x - 8)(x + 8)$ d. $(x + 16)(x - 4)$

48. Factor: $9x^2 - 25$.
    a. $(9x + 9)(x - 5)$ b. $(3x + 5)(3x - 5)$
    c. $(3x - 10)(3x - 15)$ d. $(5x + 3)(5x - 3)$

49. Factor: $16x^2 - 49y^2$.
    a. $(8x + 7)(8x - 7)$ b. $(8x + 7y)(8x - 7y)$
    c. $(4x - 7y)(4x - 7y)$ d. $(4x - 7y)(4x + 7y)$

50. Factor: $x^2 - 2x - 24$.
    a. $(x - 8)(x + 3)$ b. $(x - 12)(x + 2)$
    c. $(x - 6)(x + 4)$ d. $(x - 4)(x + 2)$

51. Factor: $x^2 + 14x + 48$.
    a. $(x + 12)(x + 4)$ b. $(x + 24)(x + 2)$
    c. $(x + 10)(x + 4)$ d. $(x + 8)(x + 6)$

52. Factor: $x^2 + 5x - 36$.
    a. $(x - 6)^2$ b. $(x + 9)(x - 4)$ c. $(x + 18)(x - 2)$ d. $(x + 10)(x - 5)$

53. Factor: $x^2 - 13x + 42$.
    a. $(x - 6)(x + 7)$
    b. $(x - 9)(x - 4)$
    c. $(x - 7)(x - 6)$
    d. $(x + 3)(x - 16)$

54. Factor: $x^2 - 6x - 16$.
    a. $(x - 8)(x + 2)$ b. $(x - 12)(x + 6)$ c. $(x - 2)(x + 8)$ d. $(x - 4)^2$

55. Which of the following trinomials will have binomial factors with the same signs?
    a. $x^2 - 6x - 16$ b. $x^2 + 10x - 24$ c. $x^2 - 12x + 20$ d. $x^2 - 4x - 32$

56. Which of the following trinomials will have binomial factors with different signs?
    a. $x^2 - 10x + 16$ b. $x^2 - 2x - 24$ c. $x^2 - 12x + 32$ d. $x^2 + 11x + 18$

SHORT ANSWER. Write the answer in the space provided.

57. Find the value of $x^2 - 7x + 18$ when $x = 6$.

    _____

58. Find the value of $(x + 9)(x - 7)$ when $x = -4$.

    _____

59. Show that $x^2 - 8x + 15 = (x - 3)(x - 5)$ is an equation by substituting $x = 9$ into both expressions.

    _____

60. Show that $x^2 - 3x - 54 = (x - 9)(x + 6)$ is an equation by substituting $x = -5$ into both expressions.

    _____

61. The surface area of a container with a radius of r is given by the function $S(r) = 15\pi r^2$. Find the surface area of the container with a radius of 5 meters.

    _____

62. The volume of a sphere with a radius of r is given by the function
    $V(r) = \dfrac{4\pi r^3}{3}$. Find the volume of a sphere with a radius of 6 feet.

    _____

63. The volume of a container with a radius of r is given by the function
    $S(r) = 10\pi r^2 + \dfrac{2\pi r^3}{3}$. Find the volume of the container with a radius
    of 9 inches.

    _____

64. Name this polynomial by using the degree and number of terms: $5x^4 - 3x + 3$.

    _____

65. Name this polynomial by using the degree and number of terms: $3x^3 + 5x$.

    _____

66. Add: $(9x^2 - 8x - 15) + (8x^2 - 2x + 20)$.

_____

67. Add: $(12x^3 - 10x + 8) + (2x^2 + 7x + 8)$.

_____

68. Subtract: $(14x^2 + 5x - 7) - (9x^2 - 6x + 2)$.

_____

69. Subtract: $(4x^3 + 2x + 5) - (6x^3 - 7x^2 - 3)$.

_____

70. Simplify: $9x^3 + 5 - 5x^2 - (9x + 8x^2 - 2x^3 + 6)$. Write your answer in standard form.

_____

71. Find the product: $6(3x + 8)$.

_____

72. Find the product: $-9(3x - 4)$.

_____

73. Find the product: $-2x(5 - 3x)$.

_____

74. Model $(x - 3)(x + 2)$ with tiles.

75. Model $(x + 4)(x - 2)$ with tiles.

76. Model $(2x - 1)(x + 3)$ with tiles.

77. Model $(3x - 2)(x - 2)$ with tiles.

78. Use the Distributive Property to find the product: $(x + 9)(x + 6)$.

_____

79. Use the Distributive Property to find the product: $(x - 7)(x - 3)$.

_____

80. Use the Distributive Property to find the product: $(x - 4)(x + 8)$.

_____

81. Use the FOIL method to find the product: $(x + 3)(x - 5)$.

_____

82. Use the FOIL method to find the product: $(5x + 4)(2x + 1)$.

_____

130

83. Use the FOIL method to find the product: $(3x - 7)(2x - 5)$.

_____

84. Use the FOIL method to find the product: $(6x + 2y)(x + 4y)$.

_____

85. Factor by removing the GCF: $16x - 24x^3$.

_____

86. Factor by removing the GCF: $9x^3 - 6x^2 + 12x^4$.

_____

87. Factor by removing the GCF: $15x^3y^4 + 10x^2y^2 - 5xy^3$.

_____

88. Write as the product of two binomials: $x(x - 8) + 4(x - 8)$.

_____

89. Write as the product of two binomials: $7(2x + 5) - 5x(2x + 5)$

_____

90. Factor: $8x + 8y + cx + cy$.

_____

91. Factor: $15xy + 6x + 20y + 8$.

_____

92. Factor: $x^2 + 10x + 25$.

_____

93. Factor: $x^2 - 16x + 64$.

_____

94. Factor: $4x^2 - 28x + 49$.

_____

95. Factor: $9x^2 + 30xy + 25y^2$.

_____

96. Factor: $x^2 - 49$.

_____

97. Factor: $16x^2 - 81$.

_____

98. Factor: $25x^2 - 49y^2$.

_____

99. Will the binomial factors of $x^2 - 7x - 144$ have the same sign or different signs?

_____

100. Factor $x^2 + 7x + 12$ with tiles.

_____

101. Factor $x^2 - 10x + 16$ with tiles.

_____

102. Factor: $x^2 - 15x + 56$.

_____

103. Factor: $x^2 + 9x - 36$.

_____

104. Factor: $x^2 - 4x - 45$.

_____

105. Factor: $x^2 + 6x - 40$.

_____

ANSWERS TO CHAPTER 7

1. Answer: c Section: 1 Objective: 1a

2. Answer: c Section: 2 Objective: 2a

3. Answer: d Section: 3 Objective: 3a

4. Answer: a Section: 4 Objective: 4a

5. Answer: b Section: 5 Objective: 5a

6. Answer: b Section: 6 Objective: 6b

7. Answer: a Section: 7 Objective: 7a

8. Answer: c. 119 Section: 1 Objective: 1a

9. Answer: b. -20 Section: 1 Objective: 1a

10. Answer: d. -26 Section: 1 Objective: 1a

11. Answer: a. 44 Section: 1 Objective: 1a

12. Answer: b. 235.6 in.^{2} Section: 1 Objective: 1b

13. Answer: c. 113.1 ft^3 Section: 1 Objective: 1b

14. Answer: d. 226.2 cm^2 Section: 1 Objective: 1b

15. Answer: c. $x^3 - 1$ Section: 2 Objective: 2a

16. Answer: b. $3x^2 - 5x + 3$ Section: 2 Objective: 2a

17. Answer: d. $9x^2 + 3x + 3$ Section: 2 Objective: 2a

18. Answer: c. $5x^3 + 6x^2 - 5x + 8$ Section: 2 Objective: 2a

19. Answer: b. $5x^2 + 7x - 7$ Section: 2 Objective: 2a

20. Answer: d. $4x^3 + 3x^2 + 8x + 6$ Section: 2 Objective: 2a

21. Answer: b. $7x^2 + 15x - 11$ Section: 2 Objective: 2a

22. Answer: d. $7x - 21$ Section: 3 Objective: 3a

23. Answer: a. $-15x - 12$ Section: 3 Objective: 3a

24. Answer: b. $5x - 2x^2$ Section: 3 Objective: 3a

25. Answer: d. $(x + 3)(x - 1) = x^2 + 2x - 3$ Section: 3 Objective: 3b

26. Answer: b. $(x - 2)(x - 3) = x^2 - 5x + 6$ Section: 3 Objective: 3b

27. Answer: c. $(2x + 1)(x - 2) = 2x^2 - 3x - 2$ Section: 3 Objective: 3b

28. Answer: d. $(2x - 3)(x - 1) = 2x^2 - 5x + 3$ Section: 3 Objective: 3b

29. Answer: d. $x^2 + 11x + 30$ Section: 4 Objective: 4a

30. Answer: b. $x^2 + 4x - 21$ Section: 4 Objective: 4a

31. Answer: c. $x^2 - 13x + 40$ Section: 4 Objective: 4a

32. Answer: a. $x^2 - 4x - 12$ Section: 4 Objective: 4b

33. Answer: c. $2x^2 + 13x - 7$ Section: 4 Objective: 4b

34. Answer: d. $6x^2 - 11x + 3$ Section: 4 Objective: 4b

35. Answer: a. $x^2 + 5xy + 6y^2$ Section: 4 Objective: 4b

36. Answer: c. $6x(2x - 3)$ Section: 5 Objective: 5a

37. Answer: b. $2x^2(2x^2 - 4x + 3)$ Section: 5 Objective: 5a

38. Answer: d. $5xy(x^2 + 2y)$ Section: 5 Objective: 5a

39. Answer: a. $(4 - x)(x + 2)$ Section: 5 Objective: 5b

40. Answer: d. $(3x + 6)(x - 5)$ Section: 5 Objective: 5b

41. Answer: b. $(5 + m)(x + y)$ Section: 5 Objective: 5b

42. Answer: c. $(2a + 5)(3b + 2)$ Section: 5 Objective: 5b

43. Answer: a. $(x + 10)^2$ Section: 6 Objective: 6a

44. Answer: d. $(x - 6)^2$ Section: 6 Objective: 6a

45. Answer: c. $(3x - 4)^2$ Section: 6 Objective: 6a

46. Answer: b. $(2x + 5y)^2$ Section: 6 Objective: 6a

47. Answer: c. $(x - 8)(x + 8)$ Section: 6 Objective: 6b

48. Answer: b. $(3x + 5)(3x - 5)$ Section: 6 Objective: 6b

49. Answer: d. $(4x - 7y)(4x + 7y)$ Section: 6 Objective: 6b

50. Answer: c. $(x - 6)(x + 4)$ Section: 7 Objective: 7b

51. Answer: d. $(x + 8)(x + 6)$ Section: 7 Objective: 7b

52. Answer: b. $(x + 9)(x - 4)$ Section: 7 Objective: 7b

53. Answer: c. $(x - 7)(x - 6)$ Section: 7 Objective: 7b

54. Answer: a. $(x - 8)(x + 2)$ Section: 7 Objective: 7b

55. Answer: c. $x^2 - 12x + 20$ Section: 7 Objective: 7b

56. Answer: b. $x^2 - 2x - 24$ Section: 7 Objective: 7b

57. Answer: 12 Section: 1 Objective: 1a

58. Answer: -55 Section: 1 Objective: 1a

59. Answer: The value of both expressions is 24. Section: 1 Objective: 1a

60. Answer: The value of both expressions is -14. Section: 1 Objective: 1a

61. Answer: $375\pi \approx 1178.1$ m^2 Section: 1 Objective: 1b

62. Answer: $288\pi \approx 904.8$ ft^3 Section: 1 Objective: 1b

63. Answer: $1296\pi \approx 4071.5$ in.^{3} Section: 1 Objective: 1b

64. Answer: trinomial of degree 4 Section: 2 Objective: 2a

65. Answer: binomial of degree 3 Section: 2 Objective: 2a

66. Answer: $17x^2 - 10x + 5$ Section: 2 Objective: 2a

67. Answer: $12x^3 + 2x^2 - 3x + 16$ Section: 2 Objective: 2a

68. Answer: $5x^2 + 11x - 9$ Section: 2 Objective: 2a

69. Answer: $-2x^3 + 7x^2 + 2x + 8$ Section: 2 Objective: 2a

70. Answer: $11x^3 - 13x^2 - 9x - 1$ Section: 2 Objective: 2a

71. Answer: $18x + 48$ Section: 3 Objective: 3a

72. Answer: $-27x + 36$ Section: 3 Objective: 3a

73. Answer: $-10x + 6x^2$ Section: 3 Objective: 3a

74. Answer: $(x - 3)(x + 2) = x^2 - x - 6$

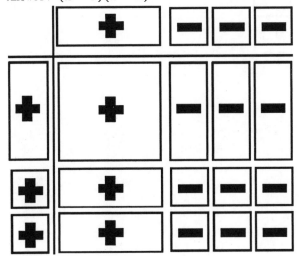

Section: 3 Objective: 3b

75. Answer: $(x + 4)(x - 2) = x^2 + 2x - 8$

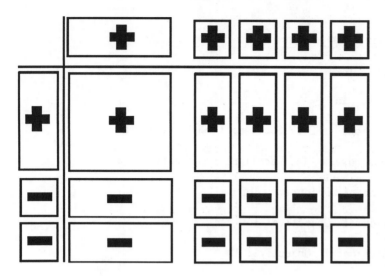

Section: 3   Objective: 3b

76. Answer: $(2x - 1)(x + 3) = 2x^2 + 5x - 3$

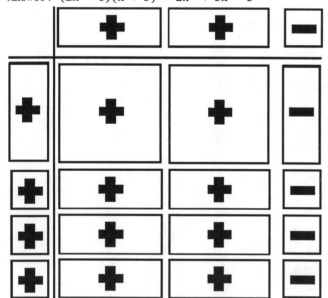

Section: 3   Objective: 3b

77. Answer: $(3x - 2)(x - 2) = 3x^2 - 8x + 4$

136

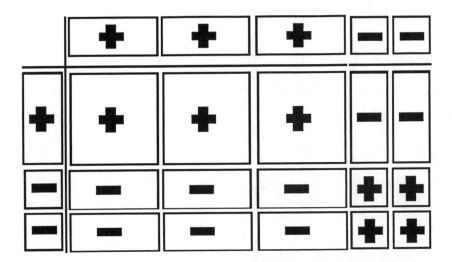

Section: 3 Objective: 3b

78. Answer: $x^2 + 15x + 54$ Section: 4 Objective: 4a

79. Answer: $x^2 - 10x + 21$ Section: 4 Objective: 4a

80. Answer: $x^2 + 4x - 32$ Section: 4 Objective: 4a

81. Answer: $x^2 - 2x - 15$ Section: 4 Objective: 4b

82. Answer: $10x^2 + 13x + 4$ Section: 4 Objective: 4b

83. Answer: $6x^2 - 29x + 35$ Section: 4 Objective: 4b

84. Answer: $6x^2 + 26xy + 8y^2$ Section: 4 Objective: 4b

85. Answer: $8x(2 - 3x^2)$ Section: 5 Objective: 5a

86. Answer: $3x^2(3x - 2 + 4x^2)$ Section: 5 Objective: 5a

87. Answer: $5xy^2(3x^2y^2 + 2x - y)$ Section: 5 Objective: 5a

88. Answer: $(x + 4)(x - 8)$ Section: 5 Objective: 5b

89. Answer: $(7 - 5x)(2x + 5)$ Section: 5 Objective: 5b

90. Answer: $(8 + c)(x + y)$ Section: 5 Objective: 5b

91. Answer: $(3x + 4)(5y + 2)$ Section: 5 Objective: 5b

92. Answer: $(x + 5)^2$ Section: 6 Objective: 6a

93. Answer: $(x - 8)^2$ Section: 6 Objective: 6a

94. Answer: $(2x - 7)^2$ Section: 6 Objective: 6a

95. Answer: $(3x + 5y)^2$ Section: 6 Objective: 6a

96. Answer: $(x + 7)(x - 7)$ Section: 6 Objective: 6b

97. Answer: $(4x - 9)(4x + 9)$ Section: 6 Objective: 6b

98. Answer: $(5x + 7y)(5x - 7y)$ Section: 6 Objective: 6b

99. Answer: different signs Section: 7 Objective: 7a

100. Answer: $(x + 4)(x + 3)$

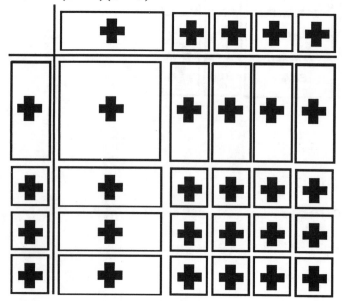

Section: 7 Objective: 7b

101. Answer: $(x - 8)(x - 2)$

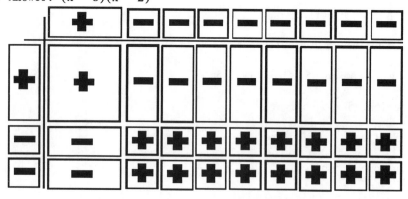

Section: 7 Objective: 7b

102. Answer: $(x - 7)(x - 8)$ Section: 7 Objective: 7b

103. Answer: $(x - 3)(x + 12)$ Section: 7 Objective: 7b

104. Answer: $(x - 9)(x + 5)$ Section: 7 Objective: 7b

105. Answer: $(x - 4)(x + 10)$ Section: 7 Objective: 7b

CHAPTER 8: Quadratic Functions

QUANTITATIVE COMPARISON

In the space provided, write:
a. if the quantity in Column A is greater than the quantity in Column B;
b. if the quantity in Column B is greater than the quantity in Column A;
c. if the two quantities are equal; or
d. if the relationship cannot be determined from the information given.

Column A	Column B	Answer

1.

| The x-coordinate of the vertex of $y = (x - 5)^2 + 3$ | The y-coordinate of the vertex of $y = (x - 5)^2 + 3$ | _____ |

2.

| The positive solution to $x^2 = 225$ | The positive solution to $x^2 = \dfrac{49}{16}$ | _____ |

3.

| The minimum value of the function $y = x^2 + 7$ | The minimum value of the function $y = x^2 + 6$ | _____ |

4.

| The larger solution to the equation $(x + 5)(x - 3) = 0$ | The larger solution to the equation $(x - 5)(x + 3) = 0$ | _____ |

5.

| The number of solutions to $3x^2 + 10x + 12 = 0$ | The number of solutions to $3x^2 + 20x + 20 = 0$ | _____ |

6.

| The largest solution to $(x + 2)(x - 3) \leq 0$ | The largest solution to $(x + 5)(x - 2) \leq 0$ | _____ |

MULTIPLE CHOICE. Circle the letter of the best answer choice.

7. Which of the following is the vertex of the graph shown?
   a. (2, 1)   b. (1, 2)   c. (0, 3)   d. (3, 0)

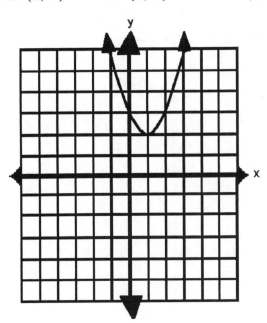

8. Which of the following is the axis of symmetry for the graph shown?
   a. $y = 2$ b. $y = 1$ c. $x = 2$ d. $x = 1$

9. What are the zeros of the function graphed?
   a. (1, 0) and (-3, 0)   b. (0, -3) and (0, 1)
   c. (-1, 0) and (3, 0)   d. (0, -1) and (0, 3)

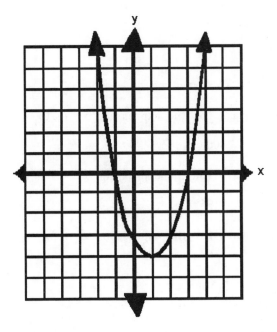

10. Which of the following is the vertex of the function $y = (x - 4)^2 + 7$?
    a. (4, 7)   b. (4, -7)   c. (-4, 7)   d. (-4, -7)

11. Which of the following is the vertex of the function $y = (x + 3)^2 - 6$?
    a. (3, 6)   b. (3, -6)   c. (-3, 6)   d. (-3, -6)

12. Which of the following is the axis of symmetry for the function $y = (x - 2)^2 + 5$?
   a. $x = -2$
   b. $x = 2$
   c. $y = -5$
   d. $y = 5$

13. Which of the following is the axis of symmetry for the function $y = (x + 3)^2 - 4$?
   a. $y = -4$
   b. $y = 4$
   c. $x = -3$
   d. $x = 3$

14.
   Which of the following is $\sqrt{\dfrac{25}{64}}$?

   a. $\dfrac{5}{64}$
   b. $\dfrac{5}{32}$
   c. $\dfrac{5}{16}$
   d. $\dfrac{5}{8}$

15. Which of the following is $\sqrt{2.56}$?
   a. 16
   b. 1.6
   c. 0.16
   d. 0.016

16. Solve for x: $x^2 = 36$.
   a. $x = \pm 1296$
   b. $x = \pm 18$
   c. $x = \pm 6$
   d. $x = \pm 4$

17. Solve for x: $x^2 = \dfrac{49}{64}$.

   a. $x = \pm\dfrac{7}{4}$
   b. $x = \pm\dfrac{7}{8}$
   c. $x = \pm\dfrac{7}{16}$
   d. $x = \pm\dfrac{7}{32}$

18. Solve for x: $x^2 = \dfrac{36}{121}$.

   a. $x = \pm\dfrac{6}{121}$
   b. $x = \pm\dfrac{18}{11}$
   c. $x = \pm\dfrac{9}{11}$
   d. $x = \pm\dfrac{6}{11}$

19. Solve for x: $(x + 3)^2 = 49$.
   a. $x = \pm 7$
   b. $x = 4$ or $x = 10$
   c. $x = 4$ or $x = -10$
   d. $x = -4$ or $x = 10$

20. Solve for x: $(x - 2)^2 + 5 = 30$.
   a. $x = 3$ or $x = 7$ b. $x = -3$ or $x = 7$ c. $x = 3$ or $x = -7$ d. $x = \pm 5$

21. Which of the following numbers will complete the square for the expression $x^2 + 20x + \underline{\quad}$?
   a. 10
   b. 20
   c. 100
   d. 400

22. Which of the following numbers will complete the square for the expression $x^2 - 14x + \underline{\quad}$?
   a. 49
   b. -49
   c. 196
   d. -196

23. Which of the following numbers will complete the square for the expression $x^2 + 5x + \underline{\quad}$?
   a. -25
   b. 25
   c. -6.25
   d. 6.25

24. Rewrite $y = x^2 + 6x + 9 - 9$ in the form $y = (x - h)^2 + k$.
   a. $y = (x + 6)^2 - 9$
   b. $y = (x + 6)^2 - 3$
   c. $y = (x + 3)^2 - 9$
   d. $y = (x + 3)^2 - 3$

25. Rewrite $y = x^2 - 12x + 36 - 36$ in the form $y = (x - h)^2 + k$.
   a. $y = (x + 6)^2 - 36$
   b. $y = (x - 6)^2 - 36$
   c. $y = (x - 6)^2 + 36$
   d. $y = (x + 6)^2 + 36$

26. Find the vertex of the function $y = x^2 - 7$.
   a. $(7, 0)$
   b. $(-7, 0)$
   c. $(0, 7)$
   d. $(0, -7)$

27. Find the minimum value of the function $y = (x - 2)^2 + 5$.
  a. 5 b. -5 c. 2 d. -2

28. Which of the following are the solutions to the equation $(x + 8)(x - 6) = 0$?
  a. $x = 8$ or $x = 6$ b. $x = 8$ or $x = -6$
  c. $x = -8$ or $x = 6$ d. $x = -8$ or $x = -6$

29. Which of the following are the solutions to the equation $(x - 5)(x + 12) = 0$?
  a. $x = 5$ or $x = 12$ b. $x = 5$ or $x = -12$
  c. $x = -5$ or $x = 12$ d. $x = -5$ or $x = -12$

30. Solve by factoring: $x^2 + 12x + 20 = 0$.
  a. $x = 2$ or $x = 10$ b. $x = -2$ or $x = -10$
  c. $x = 4$ or $x = 5$ d. $x = -4$ or $x = -5$

31. Solve by factoring: $x^2 - 3x - 18 = 0$.
  a. $x = 2$ or $x = -9$ b. $x = -2$ or $x = 9$
  c. $x = 6$ or $x = -3$ d. $x = -6$ or $x = 3$

32. Solve by completing the square: $x^2 + 2x - 15 = 0$.
  a. $x = \pm 4$ b. $x = -5$ or $x = 3$
  c. $x = 5$ or $x = -3$ d. $x = 5$ or $x = 3$

33. Solve by completing the square: $x^2 - 6x + 8 = 0$.
  a. $x = 4$ or $x = 2$ b. $x = 4$ or $x = -2$
  c. $x = -4$ or $x = 2$ d. $x = \pm 1$

34. Solve by completing the square: $x^2 + 8x + 12 = 0$.
  a. $x = \pm 2$ b. $x = \pm 6$
  c. $x = 2$ or $x = 6$ d. $x = -2$ or $x = -6$

35. Solve by using the quadratic formula: $5x^2 + 10x - 15 = 0$.
  a. $x = 3.5$ or $x = -7.5$ b. $x = -3.5$ or $x = 7.5$
  c. $x = 1$ or $x = -3$ d. $x = -1$ or $x = 3$

36. Solve by using the quadratic formula: $4x^2 + 16x + 15 = 0$.
  a. $x = -1.5$ or $x = -2.5$ b. $x = 1.5$ or $x = 2.5$
  c. $x = -4$ or $x = -6$ d. $x = 4$ or $x = 6$

37. Solve by using the quadratic formula: $2x^2 - 7x + 3 = 0$.
  a. $x = 2.5$ or $x = -7.5$ b. $x = 0.5$ or $x = 3$
  c. $x = 3$ or $x = -4$ d. $x = 4$ or $x = 6$

38. Use the quadratic formula to find the zeros of the function $y = x^2 + 12x + 27$.
  a. (0, 3) and (0, 9) b. (0, -3) and (0, -9)
  c. (3, 0) and (9, 0) d. (-3, 0) and (-9, 0)

39. Use the quadratic formula to find the zeros of the function $y = 2x^2 + 2x - 12$.
  a. (0, 2) and (0, -3) b. (0, -2) and (0, 3)
  c. (2, 0) and (-3, 0) d. (-2, 0) and (3, 0)

40. Find the value of the discriminant for the equation $4x^2 + 24x + 36 = 0$.
  a. 1152 b. 432 c. 0 d. -552

41. Use the discriminant to find how many solutions there are to the equation $2x^2 + 5x + 10 = 0$.
  a. 0 b. 1 c. 2 d. 3

42. Which of the following is a solution to the inequality $(x + 4)(x - 5) \geq 0$?
  a. -3 b. 0 c. 2 d. 7

43. Which of the following is a solution to the inequality $y > x^2 + 2x + 5$?
   a. $(0, 3)$ b. $(2, 15)$ c. $(-2, 0)$ d. $(-4, -7)$

44. Which of the following is a solution to the inequality $y \leq x^2 - 5x + 2$?
   a. $(0, 4)$ b. $(3, 0)$ c. $(5, 8)$ d. $(-3, 20)$

45. Which of the following inequalities is graphed here?
   a. $(x + 2)(x - 4) > 0$ b. $(x + 2)(x - 4) < 0$
   c. $(x - 2)(x + 4) > 0$ d. $(x - 2)(x + 4) < 0$

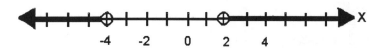

46. Which of the following inequalities is graphed here?
   a. $x^2 - 2x - 15 \leq 0$ b. $x^2 + 2x - 15 \leq 0$
   c. $x^2 - 2x - 15 \geq 0$ d. $x^2 + 2x - 15 \geq 0$

47. Which of the following inequalities is graphed here?
   a. $y \geq x^2 - 1$ b. $y \leq x^2 - 1$
   c. $y \geq x^2 + 1$ d. $y \leq x^2 + 1$

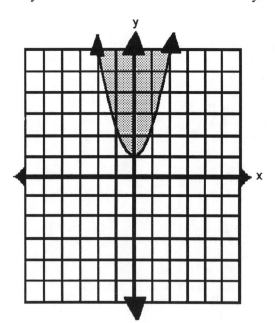

144

48. Which of the following inequalities is graphed here?
   a. $y \geq (x + 1)^2 - 3$ b. $y \leq (x + 1)^2 - 3$
   c. $y \geq (x - 1)^2 + 3$ d. $y \leq (x - 1)^2 + 3$

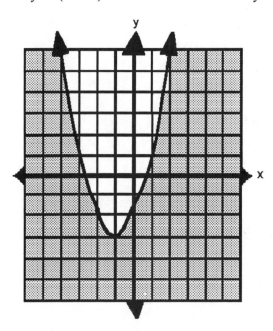

SHORT ANSWER. Write the answer in the space provided.

49. Find the vertex and the axis of symmetry for the graph shown.

_____

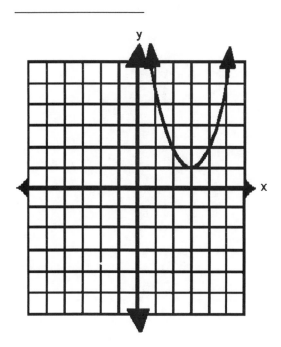

145

50. Find the vertex and the axis of symmetry for the graph shown.

_____

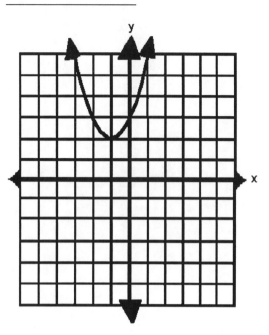

51. Graph $y = x^2 - 4x + 3$.

52. Graph $y = x^2 - 2x + 4$.

53. Find the zeros of the function graphed here.

_____

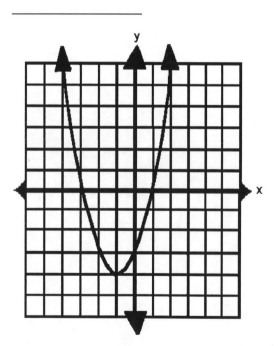

54. Find the vertex and the axis of symmetry of the function $y = (x + 5)^2 - 3$.

_____

55. Find the vertex and the axis of symmetry of the function $y = (x - 6)^2 + 4$.

_____

56. Find $\sqrt{\dfrac{81}{144}}$.

_____

57. Find $\sqrt{40.96}$.

_____

58. Solve for x: $x^2 = 121$.

_____

59. Solve for x: $x^2 = \dfrac{49}{100}$.

_____

60. Solve for x: $x^2 = 75$.

_____

61. Solve for x: $(x + 6)^2 = 144$.

_____

62. Solve for x: $(x - 7)^2 + 12 = 93$.

_____

63. Which number will complete the square for the expression
$x^2 + 24x +$ ____?

_____

64. Which number will complete the square for the expression
$x^2 - 9x +$ ____?

_____

65. Rewrite $y = x^2 + 18x + 81 - 81$ in the form $y = (x - h)^2 + k$.

_____

66. Rewrite $y = x^2 - 30x + 225 - 225$ in the form $y = (x - h)^2 + k$.

_____

67. Rewrite $y = x^2 + 10x + 32$ in the form $y = (x - h)^2 + k$.

_____

68. Find the vertex and the minimum value of the function $y = x^2 - 12$.

_____

69. Find the vertex and the minimum value of the function $y = (x - 5)^2 + 8$.

   _____

70. Solve for x: $(x + 15)(x - 3) = 0$.

   _____

71. Solve by factoring: $x^2 + 12x + 35 = 0$.

   _____

72. Solve by factoring: $x^2 - 2x - 48 = 0$.

   _____

73. Solve by factoring: $x^2 - 13x + 40 = 0$.

   _____

74. Solve by completing the square: $x^2 + 2x - 35 = 0$.

   _____

75. Solve by completing the square: $x^2 - 4x - 60 = 0$.

   _____

76. Solve by completing the square: $x^2 - 14x + 48 = 0$.

   _____

77. Solve by using the quadratic formula: $3x^2 + 3x - 36 = 0$.

   _____

78. Solve by using the quadratic formula: $8x^2 + 26x + 15 = 0$.

   _____

79. Solve by using the quadratic formula: $2x^2 - 3x - 14 = 0$.

   _____

80. Use the quadratic formula to find the zeros of the function $y = x^2 - 17x + 72$.

   _____

81. Use the quadratic formula to find the zeros of the function $y = 3x^2 + 15x + 18$.

   _____

82. Find the value of the discriminant for the equation $4x^2 + 40x + 100 = 0$.

   _____

83. Use the discriminant to find how many solutions there are to the equation $5x^2 - 9x + 4 = 0$.

   _____

84. Is (-5, 30) a solution to $y \leq x^2 - 6x + 7$?

_____

85. Solve: $(x + 3)(x - 1) \geq 0$. Graph your solution on a number line.

_____

86. Solve: $x^2 - 4x - 12 < 0$. Graph your solution on a number line.

_____

87. Solve: $x^2 - 9 \leq 0$. Graph your solution on a number line.

_____

88. Graph $y \leq x^2 - 3$. Shade the solution region.

89. Graph $y \geq (x - 1)^2 + 3$. Shade the solution region.

90. Graph $y \leq (x - 2)^2 - 4$. Shade the solution region.

ANSWERS TO CHAPTER 8

1. Answer: a   Section: 1   Objective: 1b

2. Answer: a   Section: 2   Objective: 2a

3. Answer: a   Section: 3   Objective: 3d

4. Answer: b   Section: 4   Objective: 4a

5. Answer: b   Section: 5   Objective: 5c

6. Answer: a   Section: 6   Objective: 6a

7. Answer: b. (1, 2)   Section: 1   Objective: 1a

8. Answer: d. $x = 1$ Section: 1   Objective: 1a

9. Answer: c. (-1, 0) and (3, 0)   Section: 1   Objective: 1b

10. Answer: a. (4, 7)   Section: 1   Objective: 1b

11. Answer: d. (-3, -6)   Section: 1   Objective: 1b

12. Answer: b. $x = 2$ Section: 1   Objective: 1b

13. Answer: c. $x = -3$ Section: 1   Objective: 1b

14. Answer:
    d. $\frac{5}{8}$

    Section: 2   Objective: 2a

15. Answer: b. 1.6   Section: 2   Objective: 2a

16. Answer: c. $x = \pm 6$ Section: 2   Objective: 2b

17. Answer:
    b. $x = \pm\frac{7}{8}$

    Section: 2   Objective: 2b

18. Answer:
    d. $x = \pm\frac{6}{11}$

    Section: 2   Objective: 2b

19. Answer: c. $x = 4$ and $x = -10$ Section: 2 Objective: 2b

20. Answer: b. $x = -3$ and $x = 7$ Section: 2 Objective: 2b

21. Answer: c. 100 Section: 3 Objective: 3a

22. Answer: a. 49 Section: 3 Objective: 3a

23. Answer: d. 6.25 Section: 3 Objective: 3a

24. Answer: c. $y = (x + 3)^2 - 9$ Section: 3 Objective: 3b

25. Answer: b. $y = (x - 6)^2 - 36$ Section: 3 Objective: 3b

26. Answer: d. (0, -7) Section: 3 Objective: 3c

27. Answer: a. 5 Section: 3 Objective: 3d

28. Answer: c. $x = -8$ or $x = 6$ Section: 4 Objective: 4a

29. Answer: b. $x = 5$ or $x = -12$ Section: 4 Objective: 4a

30. Answer: b. $x = -2$ or $x = -10$ Section: 4 Objective: 4a

31. Answer: c. $x = 6$ or $x = -3$ Section: 4 Objective: 4a

32. Answer: b. $x = -5$ or $x = 3$ Section: 4 Objective: 4a

33. Answer: a. $x = 4$ or $x = 2$ Section: 4 Objective: 4a

34. Answer: d. $x = -2$ or $x = -6$ Section: 4 Objective: 4a

35. Answer: c. $x = 1$ or $x = -3$ Section: 5 Objective: 5a

36. Answer: a. $x = -1.5$ or $x = -2.5$ Section: 5 Objective: 5a

37. Answer: b. $x = 0.5$ or $x = 3$ Section: 5 Objective: 5a

38. Answer: d. (-3, 0) and (-9, 0) Section: 5 Objective: 5b

39. Answer: c. (2, 0) and (-3, 0) Section: 5 Objective: 5b

40. Answer: c. 0 Section: 5 Objective: 5c

41. Answer: a. 0 Section: 5 Objective: 5c

42. Answer: d. 7 Section: 6 Objective: 6a

43. Answer: b. (2, 15) Section: 6 Objective: 6a

44. Answer: d. (-3, 20) Section: 6 Objective: 6a

45. Answer: c. $(x - 2)(x + 4) > 0$ Section: 6 Objective: 6a

46. Answer: b. $x^2 + 2x - 15 \leq 0$ Section: 6 Objective: 6a

47. Answer: c. $y \geq x^2 + 1$ Section: 6 Objective: 6a

48. Answer: b. $y \leq (x + 1)^2 - 3$ Section: 6 Objective: 6a

49. Answer: (3, 1); $x = 3$ Section: 1 Objective: 1a

50. Answer: (-1, 2); $x = -1$ Section: 1 Objective: 1a

51. Answer:

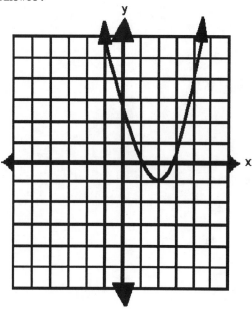

Section: 1 Objective: 1a

52. Answer:

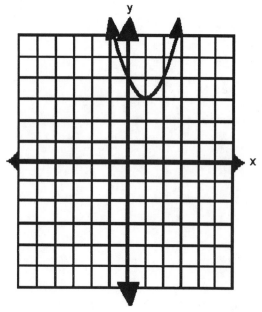

Section: 1 Objective: 1a

53. Answer: $(-3, 0)$ and $(1, 0)$ Section: 1 Objective: 1b

54. Answer: $(-5, -3)$; $x = -5$ Section: 1 Objective: 1b

55. Answer: $(6, 4)$; $x = 6$ Section: 1 Objective: 1b

56. Answer:
$$\frac{9}{12} = \frac{3}{4}$$
Section: 2 Objective: 2a

57. Answer: 6.4 Section: 2 Objective: 2a

58. Answer: $x = \pm 11$ Section: 2 Objective: 2b

59. Answer:
$$x = \pm\frac{7}{10}$$
Section: 2 Objective: 2b

60. Answer: $x \approx \pm 8.66$ Section: 2 Objective: 2b

61. Answer: $x = 6$ or $x = -18$ Section: 2 Objective: 2b

62. Answer: $x = 16$ or $x = -2$ Section: 2 Objective: 2b

63. Answer: 144 Section: 3 Objective: 3a

64. Answer: 20.25 Section: 3 Objective: 3a

65. Answer: $y = (x + 9)^2 - 81$ Section: 3 Objective: 3b

66. Answer: $y = (x - 15)^2 - 225$ Section: 3 Objective: 3b

67. Answer: $y = (x + 5)^2 + 7$ Section: 3 Objective: 3b

68. Answer: $(0, -12)$; -12 Section: 3 Objective: 3c

69. Answer: $(5, 8)$; 8 Section: 3 Objective: 3d

70. Answer: $x = -15$ or $x = 3$ Section: 4 Objective: 4a

71. Answer: $x = -5$ or $x = -7$ Section: 4 Objective: 4a

72. Answer: $x = 8$ or $x = -6$ Section: 4 Objective: 4a

73. Answer: $x = 5$ or $x = 8$ Section: 4 Objective: 4a

74. Answer: $x = 5$ or $x = -7$ Section: 4 Objective: 4a

75. Answer: $x = 10$ or $x = -6$ Section: 4 Objective: 4a

76. Answer: $x = 6$ or $x = 8$ Section: 4 Objective: 4a

77. Answer: $x = 3$ or $x = -4$ Section: 5 Objective: 5a

78. Answer: $x = -0.75$ or $x = -2.5$ Section: 5 Objective: 5a

79. Answer: $x = 3.5$ or $x = -2$ Section: 5 Objective: 5a

80. Answer: (8, 0) and (9, 0) Section: 5 Objective: 5b

81. Answer: (-3, 0) and (-2, 0) Section: 5 Objective: 5b

82. Answer: 0 Section: 5 Objective: 5c

83. Answer: Discriminant = 1; there are 2 solutions. Section: 5 Objective: 5c

84. Answer: yes Section: 6 Objective: 6a

85. Answer: $x \geq 1$ and $x \leq -3$

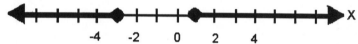

Section: 6 Objective: 6a

86. Answer: $-2 < x < 6$

Section: 6 Objective: 6a

87. Answer: $-3 \leq x \leq 3$

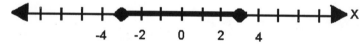

Section: 6 Objective: 6a

88. Answer:

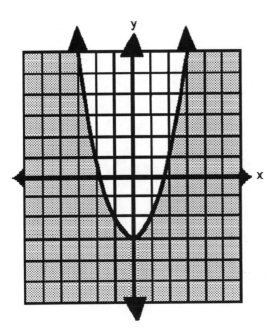

Section: 6 Objective: 6a

89. Answer:

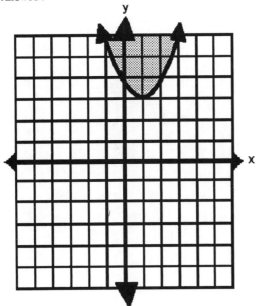

Section: 6 Objective: 6a

155

90. Answer:

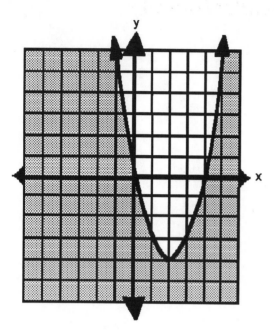

Section: 6 Objective: 6a

CHAPTER 9:   *Radicals and Coordinate Geometry*

QUANTITATIVE COMPARISON

In the space provided, write:
a. if the quantity in Column A is greater than the quantity in Column B;
b. if the quantity in Column B is greater than the quantity in Column A;
c. if the two quantities are equal; or
d. if the relationship cannot be determined from the information given.

Column A	Column B	Answer

1.

$$\sqrt{\frac{16}{25}}$$

$$\sqrt{\frac{25}{36}}$$

_____

2.

$$\sqrt{6}\,\sqrt{8}$$

$$\sqrt{4}\,\sqrt{12}$$

_____

3.

The solution to
$$\sqrt{x + 7} = 3$$

The solution to
$$\sqrt{x + 12} = 5$$

_____

4.

The length of side x

The length of side y

_____

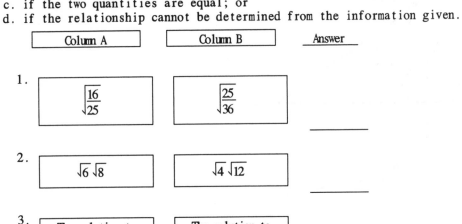

5.

The distance between (3, 6) and (7, 6)	The distance between (4, 2) and (4, 5)

_____

6.

The radius of the
circle with the
equation
$$(x + 6)^2 + (y + 8)^2 = 16$$

The radius of the
circle with the
equation
$$x^2 + y^2 = 18$$

_____

7.

| tan ∠A | | tan ∠B | | _____ |

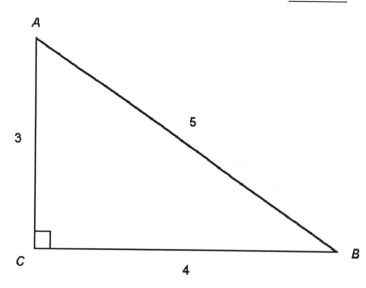

8.

| sin ∠A | | cos ∠B | | _____ |

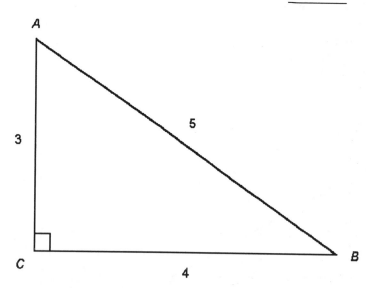

MULTIPLE CHOICE. Circle the letter of the best answer choice.

9. Which of the following is an irrational number?

   a. $\sqrt{0.25}$ b. $\sqrt{169}$ c. $\sqrt{23}$ d. $\sqrt{\dfrac{9}{25}}$

10. Find the length of a side of the square with an area of 196 cm^2.
    a. 98 cm   b. 49 cm   c. 14 cm   d. 7 cm

11. Find the length of a side of the square with an area of 40 in.^{2}.
    a. 10 in.   b. 6.32 in.   c. 5 in.   d. 4.47 in.

12. Which of the following functions is graphed here?

a. $y = \sqrt{x + 2}$ b. $y = \sqrt{x - 2}$ c. $y = \sqrt{x} + 2$ d. $y = \sqrt{x} - 2$

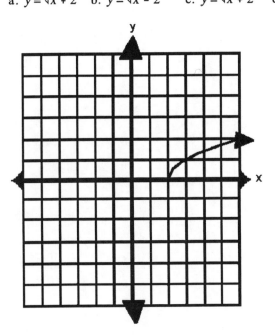

13. Which of the following functions is graphed here?

a. $y = \sqrt{x + 3}$ b. $y = \sqrt{x - 3}$ c. $y = \sqrt{x} + 3$ d. $y = \sqrt{x} - 3$

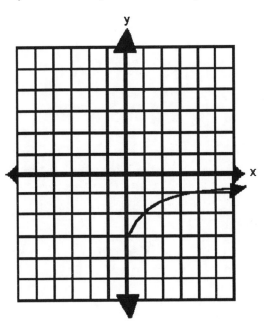

14. Which of the following functions is graphed here?

   a. $y=\sqrt{x-1}$ b. $y=\sqrt{x}-1$ c. $y=-\sqrt{x}$ d. $y=\sqrt{-x}$

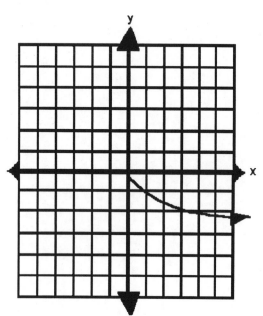

15. Identify the positive and negative square roots of 0.16.

   a. ±0.8   b. ±0.08   c. ±0.4   d. ±0.04

16. Write in simple radical form: $\sqrt{50}$.

   a. $25\sqrt{2}$ b. $2\sqrt{25}$ c. $5\sqrt{2}$ d. $2\sqrt{5}$

17. Write in simple radical form: $\sqrt{a^{16}b^{10}}$.

   a. a^4b^5 b. a^8b^5 c. $a^4b^3\sqrt{b}$ d. $a^8b^3\sqrt{b}$

18. Simplify: $\sqrt{3}\sqrt{27}$.

   a. 27   b. $\sqrt{30}$ c. 9   d. $\sqrt{91}$

19. Simplify: $\dfrac{\sqrt{60}}{\sqrt{15}}$.

   a. $\sqrt{45}$ b. 45   c. $\sqrt{2}$ d. 2

20. Add: $3\sqrt{2} + 5\sqrt{2} + 2\sqrt{2}$.

   a. $20\sqrt{2}$ b. $10\sqrt{2}$ c. $10\sqrt{6}$ d. 20

21. Simplify: $(2\sqrt{3})^2$.

   a. $4\sqrt{6}$ b. 12   c. $4\sqrt{3}$ d. 6

22. Multiply: $(\sqrt{6} + 3)(\sqrt{6} - 3)$.

   a. $\sqrt{12} - 9$ b. $6\sqrt{6} - 9$ c. 25   d. -3

23. Solve for x: $\sqrt{x-5} = 9$.

   a. $x = 86$ b. $x = 76$ c. $x = 23$ d. $x = 8$

24. Solve for x: $\sqrt{2x} = 16$.
    a. $x = 8$ b. $x = 16$ c. $x = 64$ d. $x = 128$

25. Solve for x: $\sqrt{4x + 9} = 7$.
    a. $x = 4$ b. $x = 10$ c. $x = 14$ d. $x = 21$

26. Solve for x: $\sqrt{4x - 3} = x$.
    a. $x = -1$ or $x = 3$ b. $x = 1$ or $x = -3$
    c. $x = 1$ or $x = 3$ d. $x = -1$ or $x = -3$

27. Solve for x: $2x^2 = 72$.
    a. $x = \pm18$ b. $x = \pm9$ c. $x = \pm12$ d. $x = \pm6$

28. Solve for x: $4x^2 = 256$.
    a. $x = \pm4$ b. $x = \pm8$ c. $x = \pm32$ d. $x = \pm128$

29. Solve for x: $8x^2 - 4 = 196$.
    a. $x = \pm2.25$ b. $x = \pm4.9$ c. $x = \pm5$ d. $x = \pm40$

30. Find the length of the third side of the triangle shown.
    a. 17 cm   b. 23 cm   c. 169 cm   d. 289 cm

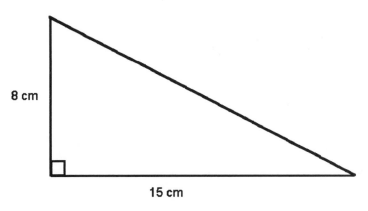

8 cm

15 cm

31. Find the length of the third side of the triangle shown.
    a. 25.6 cm   b. 16 cm   c. 12 cm   d. 7.8 cm

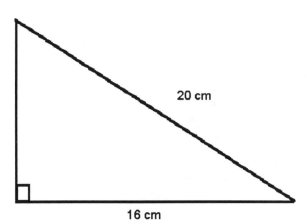

20 cm

16 cm

32. Find the approximate length of the third side of the triangle shown.
    a. 21.6 in.   b. 18 in.   c. 12.8 in.   d. 6 in.

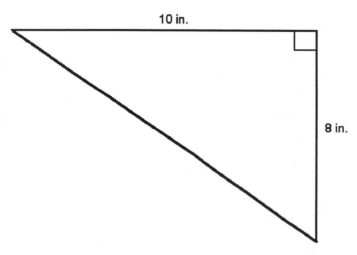

10 in.

8 in.

33. Find the approximate length of the third side of the triangle shown.
    a. 19.3 in.   b. 16.6 in.   c. 12.4 in.   d. 11 in.

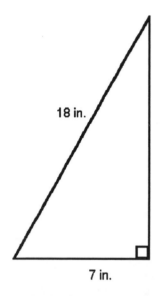

18 in.

7 in.

34. A hiker leaves camp and walks 5 miles east. The hiker then walks 12 miles south. How far from camp is the hiker?
    a. 6.8 miles   b. 7 miles   c. 10.9 miles   d. 13 miles

35. A boat leaves port and travels 15 miles east. The boat then travels north. If the boat stops when it is 35 miles from port, how far north did the boat travel?
    a. 50 miles   b. 38.1 miles   c. 31.6 miles   d. 24.8 miles

36. Find the diagonal of the square with sides of 8 cm.
    a. 4 cm   b. 5.7 cm   c. 8.6 cm   d. 11.3 cm

37. Find the distance between (2, 5) and (8, 13).
    a. 8   b. 10   c. 14   d. 25

38. Find the distance between (2, 9) and (6, 20).
    a. 3.9   b. 7.1   c. 11.7   d. 15.7

39. A triangle with which of the following three sides is a right triangle?
    a. 4, 5, 6   b. 8, 15, 17   c. 10, 12, 16   d. 6, 9, 12

40. A triangle with which of the following three sides is *not* a right triangle?
    a. 9, 12, 15   b. 7, 24, 25   c. 10, 15, 20   d. 15, 20, 25

41. Find the midpoint of the segment with endpoints at (4, 10) and (8, 12).
    a. (7, 10)   b. (8, 9)   c. (18, 22)   d. (6, 11)

42. Find the midpoint of the segment with endpoints at (-7, -9) and (13, -11).
    a. (-8, -1)   b. (3, -10)   c. (-9, 2)   d. (-3, 1)

43. M is the midpoint of $\overline{AB}$. If A has coordinates of (6, 8) and M has coordinates of (11, 14), what are the coordinates of B?
    a. (8.5, 11)   b. (7, 12.5)   c. (16, 20)   d. (14, 25)

44. Which of the following is the equation of the circle with its center at (2, 3) and a radius of 9?
    a. $(x + 2)^2 + (y + 3)^2 = 3$ b. $(x - 2)^2 + (y - 3)^2 = 3$
    c. $(x + 2)^2 + (y + 3)^2 = 81$ d. $(x - 2)^2 + (y - 3)^2 = 81$

45. Which of the following is the equation of the circle with its center at (3, -5) and a radius of 16?
    a. $(x + 3)^2 + (y - 5)^2 = 4$ b. $(x - 3)^2 + (y + 5)^2 = 4$
    c. $(x - 3)^2 + (y + 5)^2 = 256$ d. $(x + 3)^2 + (y - 5)^2 = 256$

46. Find the center and radius of the circle with the equation $(x - 5)^2 + (y - 2)^2 = 4$.
    a. center at (5, 2) and radius of 2
    b. center at (5, 2) and radius of 16
    c. center at (-5, -2) and radius of 2
    d. center at (-5, -2) and radius of 16

47. Find the center and radius of the circle with the equation $(x + 8)^2 + (y - 6)^2 = 36$.
    a. center at (-8, 6) and radius of 1296
    b. center at (8, -6) and radius of 1296
    c. center at (-8, 6) and radius of 6
    d. center at (8, -6) and radius of 6

48. Find the center and radius of the circle with the equation $(x - 7)^2 + y^2 = 10$.
    a. center at (7, 1) and radius of 100
    b. center at (7, -1) and radius of $\sqrt{10}$
    c. center at (7, 0) and radius of 5
    d. center at (7, 0) and radius of $\sqrt{10}$

49. Find the approximate length of the diagonal of the rectangle shown.
   a. 7   b. 5   c. 8.6   d. 7.1

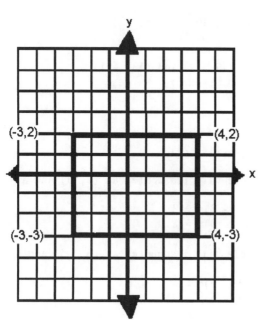

50. Find the approximate length of the diagonal of the rectangle shown.
   a. 3.6   b. 8.5   c. 3   d. 8

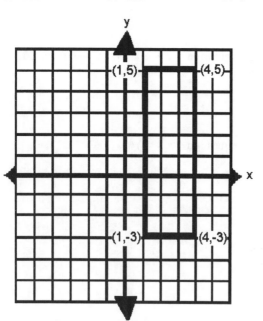

51. Which of the following is tan $\angle B$?

    a. $\dfrac{8}{15}$ b. $\dfrac{8}{17}$ c. $\dfrac{15}{8}$ d. $\dfrac{17}{8}$

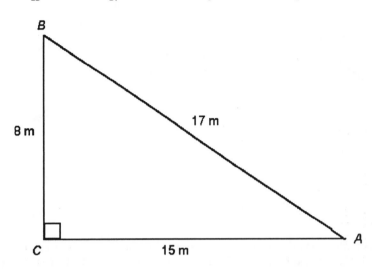

52. Which of the following is the measure of $\angle A$?

    a. 25°   b. 28°   c. 41°   d. 62°

53. If tan $\angle A = 1$, what is the measure of $\angle A$?

    a. 0.02°   b. 1°   c. 45°   d. 90°

54. Find x.

    a. 12.5 cm   b. 17 cm   c. 10.6 cm   d. 32 cm

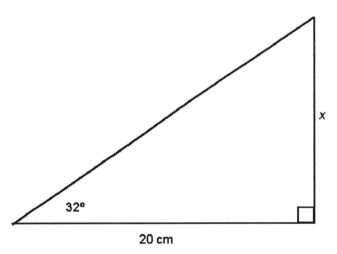

55. Find the approximate length of side x.
   a. 47.7 in.   b. 35.8 in.   c. 33.6 in.   d. 25.2 in.

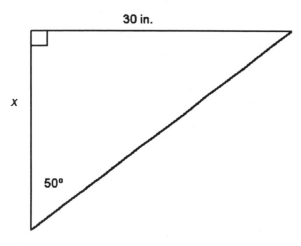

30 in.

x

50°

56. A tower is held in place by wires. The wires are attached to the ground at a point 10 feet from the bottom of the tower, and the wires form a 70° angle with the ground. How high up on the tower are the wires attached?
   a. 3.6 ft   b. 17.3 ft   c. 27.5 ft   d. 36.4 ft

57. A ramp leading to a stage forms a 15° angle with the ground. The ramp starts at a point 18 feet from the base of the stage. How high is the stage?
   a. 3.7 ft   b. 4.8 ft   c. 17.4 ft   d. 67.2 ft

58. Find the approximate length of side x.
   a. 8.6 cm   b. 10.5 cm   c. 12.28 cm   d. 26.2 cm

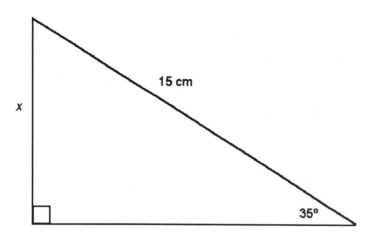

15 cm

x

35°

59. Find the approximate length of side x.
    a. 49.1 in.   b. 22.3 in.   c. 16.8 in.   d. 11.3 in.

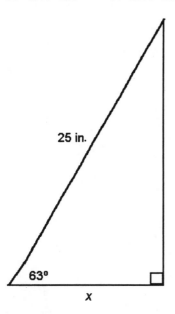

60. Find the measure of ∠A.
    a. 31.6°   b. 38°   c. 52°   d. 58.4°

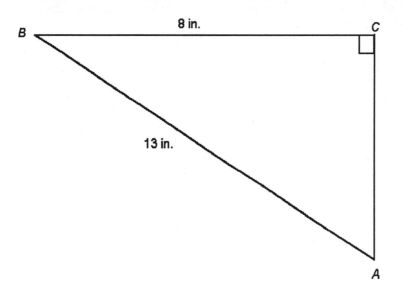

61. Find the measure of ∠B.
   a. 33°   b. 40°   c. 50°   d. 57°

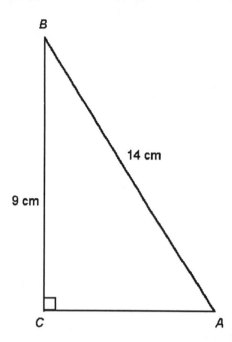

62. A kite string forms an angle of 65° with the ground. How much string is needed for the kite to reach a height of 50 feet?
   a. 45.3 ft   b. 55.2 ft   c. 107.2 ft   d. 118.3 ft

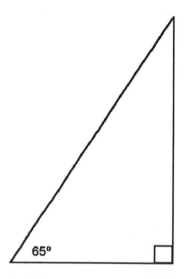

63. Cables that are 30 feet long are attached to a tower at a point 20 ft above the ground. The cables are also anchored in the ground. What angle do the cables make with the ground?
   a. 33.7°   b. 41.8°   c. 48.2°   d. 56.3°

64. A ladder is leaning against a house. The bottom of the ladder is 4 feet from the house, and the ladder forms a 70.5° angle with the ground. How long is the ladder?
   a. 10 ft   b. 11 ft   c. 12 ft   d. 13 ft

SHORT ANSWER. Write the answer in the space provided.

65. Find the length of a side of a square with an area of 289 m².

_____

66. Find the length of a side of a square with an area of 60 ft^2.

_____

67. Graph $y = \sqrt{x + 3}$.

68. Graph $y = \sqrt{x} + 2$.

69. Graph $y = -\sqrt{x - 1}$.

70. Identify the positive and negative square roots for 42.

_____

71. Identify the positive and negative square roots for 0.36.

_____

72. Write $\sqrt{45}$ in simple radical form.

_____

73. Write $\sqrt{a^8 b^{12}}$ in simple radical form.

_____

74. Simplify: $\dfrac{\sqrt{72}}{\sqrt{8}}$.

_____

75. Simplify: $6\sqrt{3} + 3\sqrt{3} - 5\sqrt{3}$.

_____

76. Simplify: $(5\sqrt{7})^2$.

_____

77. Simplify: $\sqrt{6}(\sqrt{7} + 4)$.

_____

78. Simplify: $(3 - \sqrt{7})(3 + \sqrt{7})$.

_____

79. Solve for x: $\sqrt{x + 12} = 8$.

_____

80. Solve for x: $\sqrt{5x} = 15$.

_____

81. Solve for x: $\sqrt{3x - 15} = 9$.

_____

82. Solve for x: $\sqrt{6x - 8} = x$.

_____

83. Solve for x: $5x^2 = 245$.

_____

84. Solve for x: $8x^2 = 648$.

_____

85. Solve for x: $3x^2 - 7 = 500$

_____

86. Find the length of the third side of this triangle.

_____

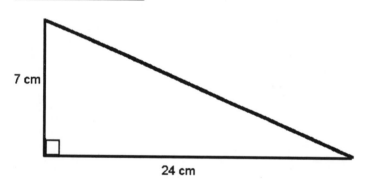

7 cm

24 cm

87. Find the length of the third side of this triangle.

_____

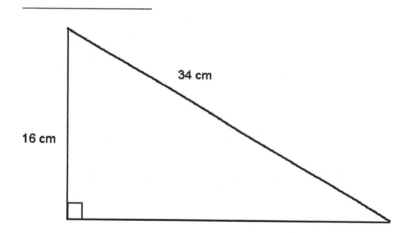

34 cm

16 cm

88. Find the length of the third side of this triangle.

_____

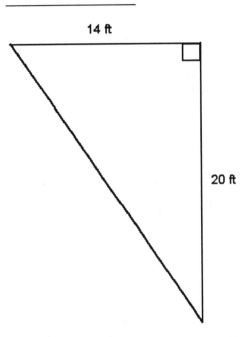

89. Find the length of the third side of this triangle.

_____

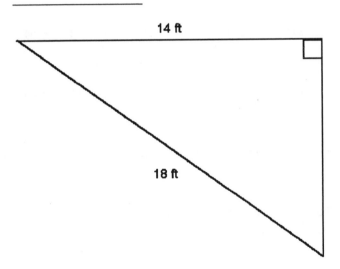

90. A bus leaves the station and travels 25 miles east. The bus then turns south and travels 45 miles. How far from the station is the bus?

_____

91. A hiker leaves camp and walks 2.4 miles east. The hiker then turns north and walks until he is 3 miles from camp. How far north did the hiker walk?

_____

92. Find the diagonal of the square with sides of 12 in.

_____

93. Find the distance between (6, 5) and (15, 17).

_____

94. Find the distance between (8, 10) and (11, 5).

_____

95. Is a triangle with sides of 12, 15, and 18 a right triangle? Explain.

_____

96. Is a triangle with sides of 1.4, 4.8, and 5 a right triangle? Explain.

_____

97. Find the midpoint of the segment with endpoints at (7, 4) and (17, 12).

_____

98. Find the midpoint of the segment with endpoints at (-12, -9) and (2, -5).

_____

99. M is the midpoint of $\overline{AB}$. If A has coordinates of (5, -2) and M has coordinates of (11, 6), what are the coordinates of B?

_____

100. Write the center and radius of the circle with the equation $(x - 6)^2 + (y + 12)^2 = 64$.

_____

101. Write the center and radius of the circle with the equation $(x + 4)^2 + (y - 15)^2 = 20$.

_____

102. Write the equation of the circle with its center at (-8, 3) and a radius of 9.

_____

103. Write the equation of the circle with its center at (10, -5) and a radius of $\sqrt{15}$.

_____

104. Write the equation of the circle with its center at (0, 9) and a radius of 25.

_____

105. Find the length of the diagonal of the rectangle shown.

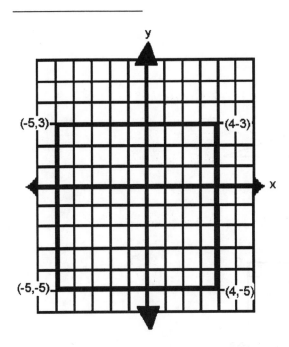

106. Find the length of the diagonal of the rectangle shown.

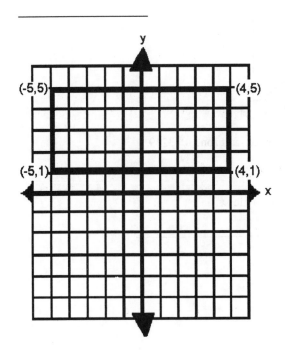

107. Find tan ∠A and tan ∠B.

_____

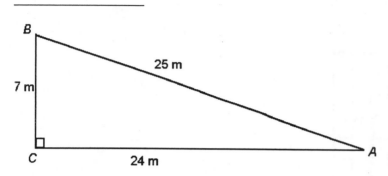

108. Find the measure of ∠A.

_____

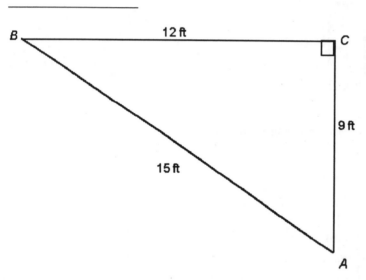

109. Find the corresponding angle for this tangent approximation: 0.3249.

_____

110. Write and solve an equation to find the length of side x.

_____

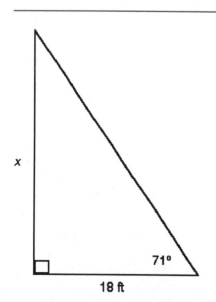

111. Write and solve an equation to find the length of side *x*.

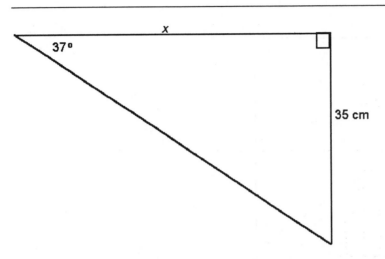

112. A ladder leaning against a wall reaches a point 8 feet up the wall. If the ladder makes a 27° angle with the wall, how far from the bottom of the wall is the bottom of the ladder? Write and solve an equation to represent the problem.

113. A surveyor measures the angle to the top of a building as 18°. If the surveyor is 200 feet from the bottom of the building, how tall is the building? Write and solve an equation to represent the problem.

114. Write and solve an equation to find the length of side *x*.

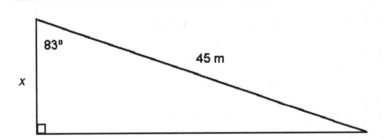

115. Write and solve an equation to find the length of side *x*.

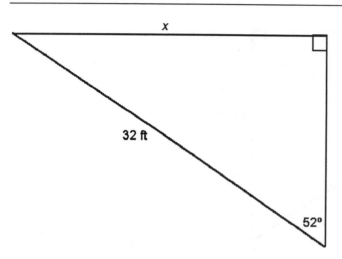

116. Write and solve an equation to find the measure of ∠A.

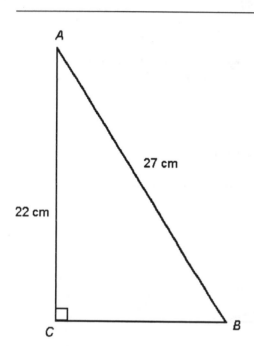

117. Write and solve an equation to find the measure of ∠A.

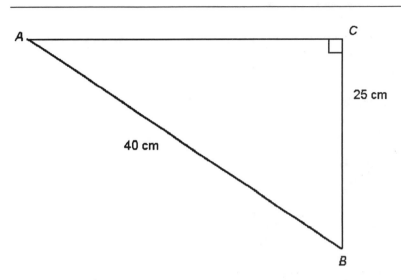

118. An advertising blimp is attached to the ground by a cable that forms a 78° angle with the ground. If the blimp is flying 65 feet above the ground, how long is the cable attaching it to the ground? Write and solve an equation to represent the problem.

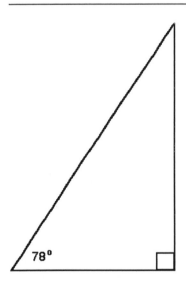

119. A playground slide starts at a point 10 feet above the ground. The slide makes an angle of 52° with the ground. About how long is the slide? Write and solve an equation to represent the problem.

120. A moving van comes with an 8-foot ramp. If the body of the moving van is 3 feet off the ground, about what angle does the ramp make with the ground? Write and solve an equation to represent the problem.

ANSWERS TO CHAPTER 9

1. Answer: b Section: 1 Objective: 1c

2. Answer: c Section: 2 Objective: 2b

3. Answer: b Section: 3 Objective: 3a

4. Answer: b Section: 4 Objective: 4a

5. Answer: a Section: 5 Objective: 5a

6. Answer: b Section: 6 Objective: 6a

7. Answer: a Section: 7 Objective: 7a

8. Answer: c Section: 8 Objective: 8a

9. Answer:
   c. $\sqrt{23}$
   Section: 1 Objective: 1a

10. Answer: c. 14 cm Section: 1 Objective: 1a

11. Answer: b. 6.32 in. Section: 1 Objective: 1a

12. Answer:
    b. $y = \sqrt{x - 2}$
    Section: 1 Objective: 1b

13. Answer:
    d. $y = \sqrt{x} - 3$
    Section: 1 Objective: 1b

14. Answer:
    c. $y = -\sqrt{x}$
    Section: 1 Objective: 1b

15. Answer: c. ±0.4 Section: 1 Objective: 1c

16. Answer:
    c. $5\sqrt{2}$
    Section: 2 Objective: 2a

17. Answer: b. $a^8 b^5$ Section: 2 Objective: 2a

18. Answer: c. 9 Section: 2 Objective: 2b

19. Answer: d. 2 Section: 2 Objective: 2b

20. Answer:
    b. $10\sqrt{2}$
    Section: 2 Objective: 2b

21. Answer: b. 12 Section: 2 Objective: 2b

22. Answer: d. -3 Section: 2 Objective: 2b

23. Answer: a. $x = 86$ Section: 3 Objective: 3a

24. Answer: d. $x = 128$ Section: 3 Objective: 3a

25. Answer: b. $x = 10$ Section: 3 Objective: 3a

26. Answer: c. $x = 1$ or $x = 3$ Section: 3 Objective: 3a

27. Answer: d. $x = \pm6$ Section: 3 Objective: 3b

28. Answer: b. $x = \pm8$ Section: 3 Objective: 3b

29. Answer: c. $x = \pm5$ Section: 3 Objective: 3b

30. Answer: a. 17 cm   Section: 4 Objective: 4a

31. Answer: c. 12 cm Section: 4 Objective: 4a

32. Answer: c. 12.8 in.   Section: 4 Objective: 4a

33. Answer: b. 16.6 in.   Section: 4 Objective: 4a

34. Answer: d. 13 miles Section: 4 Objective: 4b

35. Answer: c. 31.6 miles Section: 4 Objective: 4b

36. Answer: d. 11.3 cm Section: 4 Objective: 4b

37. Answer: b. 10 Section: 5 Objective: 5a

38. Answer: c. 11.7 Section: 5 Objective: 5a

39. Answer: b. 8, 15, 17 Section: 5 Objective: 5b

40. Answer: c. 10, 15, 20 Section: 5 Objective: 5b

41. Answer: d. (6, 11) Section: 5 Objective: 5c

42. Answer: b. (3, -10) Section: 5 Objective: 5c

43. Answer: c. (16, 20) Section: 5 Objective: 5c

44. Answer: d. $(x - 2)^2 + (y - 3)^2 = 81$ Section: 6 Objective: 6a

45. Answer: c. $(x - 3)^2 + (y + 5)^2 = 256$ Section: 6 Objective: 6a

46. Answer: a. center at (5, 2) and radius of 2 Section: 6 Objective: 6a

47. Answer: c. center at (-8, 6) and radius of 6 Section: 6 Objective: 6a

48. Answer:
   d. center at (7, 0) and radius of $\sqrt{10}$
   Section: 6 Objective: 6a

49. Answer: c. 8.6   Section: 6 Objective: 6b

50. Answer: b. 8.5 Section: 6 Objective: 6b

51. Answer:
   c. $\dfrac{15}{8}$
   Section: 7 Objective: 7a

52. Answer: b. 28°   Section: 7 Objective: 7a

53. Answer: c. 45°   Section: 7 Objective: 7a

54. Answer: a. 12.5 cm Section: 7 Objective: 7b

55. Answer: d. 25.2 in. Section: 7 Objective: 7b

56. Answer: c. 27.5 ft Section: 7 Objective: 7b

57. Answer: b. 4.8 ft Section: 7 Objective: 7b

58. Answer: a. 8.6 cm Section: 8 Objective: 8a

59. Answer: d. 11.3 in. Section: 8 Objective: 8a

60. Answer: b. 38°   Section: 8 Objective: 8a

61. Answer: c. 50°   Section: 8 Objective: 8a

62. Answer: b. 55.2 ft Section: 8 Objective: 8a

63. Answer: b. 41.8° Section: 8 Objective: 8a

64. Answer: c. 12 ft Section: 8 Objective: 8a

65. Answer: 17 m Section: 1 Objective: 1a

66. Answer:
   $\sqrt{60} \approx 7.75$ ft
   Section: 1 Objective: 1a

67. Answer:

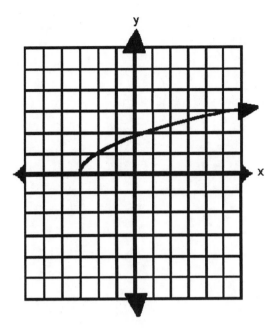

Section: 1   Objective: 1b

68. Answer:

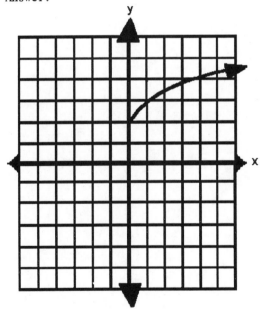

Section: 1   Objective: 1b

69. Answer:

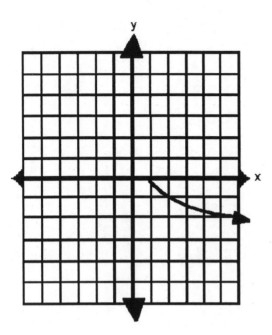

Section: 1 Objective: 1b

70. Answer: ≈ ±6.48 Section: 1 Objective: 1c

71. Answer: ±0.6 Section: 1 Objective: 1c

72. Answer:

$3\sqrt{5}$

Section: 2 Objective: 2a

73. Answer: $a^4 b^6$ Section: 2 Objective: 2a

74. Answer: 3 Section: 2 Objective: 2b

75. Answer:

$4\sqrt{3}$

Section: 2 Objective: 2b

76. Answer: 175 Section: 2 Objective: 2b

77. Answer:

$\sqrt{42} + 4\sqrt{6}$

Section: 2 Objective: 2b

78. Answer: 2 Section: 2 Objective: 2b

79. Answer: $x = 52$ Section: 3   Objective: 3a

80. Answer: $x = 45$ Section: 3   Objective: 3a

81. Answer: $x = 32$ Section: 3   Objective: 3a

82. Answer: $x = 2$ or $x = 4$ Section: 3   Objective: 3a

83. Answer: $x = \pm7$ Section: 3   Objective: 3b

84. Answer: $x = \pm9$ Section: 3   Objective: 3b

85. Answer: $x = \pm13$ Section: 3   Objective: 3b

86. Answer: 25 cm   Section: 4   Objective: 4a

87. Answer: 30 cm   Section: 4   Objective: 4a

88. Answer: ≈ 24.41 ft   Section: 4   Objective: 4a

89. Answer: ≈ 11.3 ft   Section: 4   Objective: 4a

90. Answer: About 51.48 miles   Section: 4   Objective: 4b

91. Answer: 1.8 miles   Section: 4   Objective: 4b

92. Answer:
    $12\sqrt{2} \approx 16.97$ in.
    Section: 4   Objective: 4b

93. Answer: 15   Section: 5   Objective: 5a

94. Answer:
    $\sqrt{34} \approx 5.83$
    Section: 5   Objective: 5a

95. Answer: No; $12^2 + 15^2 \neq 18^2$ Section: 5   Objective: 5b

96. Answer: Yes; $1.4^2 + 4.8^2 = 5^2$ Section: 5   Objective: 5b

97. Answer: (12, 8)   Section: 5   Objective: 5c

98. Answer: (-5, -7)   Section: 5   Objective: 5c

99. Answer: (17, 14)   Section: 5   Objective: 5c

100. Answer: (6, -12); 8   Section: 6   Objective: 6a

101. Answer:
     (-4, 15); $\sqrt{20} \approx 4.47$
     Section: 6   Objective: 6a

102. Answer: $(x + 8)^2 + (y - 3)^2 = 81$ Section: 6   Objective: 6a

103. Answer: $(x - 10)^2 + (y + 5)^2 = 15$ Section: 6   Objective: 6a

104. Answer: $x^2 + (y - 9)^2 = 625$ Section: 6   Objective: 6a

105. Answer:
$\sqrt{145} \approx 12.04$
Section: 6   Objective: 6b

106. Answer:
$\sqrt{97} \approx 9.85$
Section: 6   Objective: 6b

107. Answer:
$\tan \angle A = \dfrac{7}{24}$, $\tan \angle B = \dfrac{24}{7}$
Section: 7   Objective: 7a

108. Answer: about $53.13°$ Section: 7   Objective: 7a

109. Answer: $18°$ Section: 7   Objective: 7a

110. Answer:
$\tan 71° = \dfrac{x}{18}$, $x \approx 52.28$ ft
Section: 7   Objective: 7b

111. Answer:
$\tan 37° = \dfrac{35}{x}$, $x \approx 46.45$ cm
Section: 7   Objective: 7b

112. Answer:
$\tan 27° = \dfrac{x}{8}$, $x \approx 4.08$ ft
Section: 7   Objective: 7b

113. Answer:
$\tan 18° = \dfrac{x}{200}$, $x \approx 64.98$; about 65 feet tall
Section: 7   Objective: 7b

114. Answer:

$\cos 83° = \dfrac{x}{45}$, $x \approx 5.48$ m

Section: 8   Objective: 8a

115. Answer:

$\sin 52° = \dfrac{x}{32}$, $x \approx 25.22$ ft

Section: 8   Objective: 8a

116. Answer:

$\cos \angle A = \dfrac{22}{27}$, $m\angle A \approx 35.43°$

Section: 8   Objective: 8a

117. Answer:

$\sin \angle A = \dfrac{25}{40}$, $m\angle A \approx 38.68°$

Section: 8   Objective: 8a

118. Answer:

$\sin 78° = \dfrac{65}{x}$, $x \approx 66.45$; about 66.45 ft

Section: 8   Objective: 8a

119. Answer:

$\sin 52° = \dfrac{10}{x}$, $x \approx 12.69$; about 12.69 ft

Section: 8   Objective: 8a

120. Answer:

$\sin x = \dfrac{3}{8}$, $x \approx 22.02$; about 22°

Section: 8   Objective: 8a

CHAPTER 10: *Rational Functions*

QUANTITATIVE COMPARISON

In the space provided, write:
a. if the quantity in Column A is greater than the quantity in Column B;
b. if the quantity in Column B is greater than the quantity in Column A;
c. if the two quantities are equal; or
d. if the relationship cannot be determined from the information given.

Column A	Column B	Answer

1.

The value of $\dfrac{5x + 1}{2x}$ when $x = 2$	The value of $\dfrac{5x}{2x + 1}$ when $x = 2$

_____

2. Suppose that y varies inversely as x and that y is 15 when x is 27.

y when x is 23	y when x is 31

_____

3.   For a given value of x:

$\dfrac{x + y}{(x - y)(x + y)}$	$\dfrac{3}{3x - 3y}$

_____

4.   For a given value of x:

$\dfrac{3}{2x} \cdot \dfrac{x}{2}$	$\dfrac{x - 2}{4} \cdot \dfrac{2}{x - 2}$

_____

5.

The solution to $\dfrac{2}{x} + \dfrac{4}{x} = \dfrac{3}{4}$	The solution to $\dfrac{3}{x} + \dfrac{5}{x} = \dfrac{2}{3}$

_____

6.

The solution to $\dfrac{x}{12} = \dfrac{72}{96}$	The solution to $\dfrac{3}{17} = \dfrac{x}{68}$

_____

7.   For given values of a, b, and c:

$(a + b) + c$	$b + (a + c)$

_____

MULTIPLE CHOICE. Circle the letter of the best answer choice.

8. Evaluate $\dfrac{x^2 + 6}{x^2 + 1}$ when $x = 2$.

   a. 6   b. 5   c. 2   d. undefined

186

10. For which values of x is $\dfrac{x-5}{x+3}$ undefined?

   a. $x = 3$ b. $x = -3$ c. $x = 5$ d. $x = -5$

11. For which values of x is $\dfrac{x^2-4}{(x+5)(x-1)}$ undefined?

   a. $x = \pm 2$ b. $x = \pm 4$
   c. $x = 5$ or $x = -1$ d. $x = -5$ or $x = 1$

12. Which of the following functions is graphed here?

   a. $f(x) = \dfrac{1}{x+2}$ b. $f(x) = \dfrac{1}{x-2}$ c. $f(x) = \dfrac{1}{x} + 2$ d. $f(x) = \dfrac{1}{x} - 2$

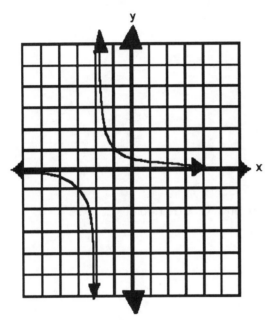

13. Which of the following functions is graphed here?

   a. $f(x) = \dfrac{1}{x+2} - 1$ b. $f(x) = \dfrac{1}{x-2} - 1$

   c. $f(x) = \dfrac{1}{x-1} + 2$ d. $f(x) = \dfrac{1}{x-1} - 2$

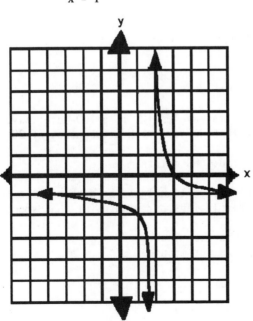

14. Which of the following functions is graphed here?

    a. $f(x) = \dfrac{1}{x-1}$ b. $f(x) = \dfrac{1}{x} - 1$ c. $f(x) = \dfrac{-2}{x}$ d. $f(x) = \dfrac{-x}{2}$

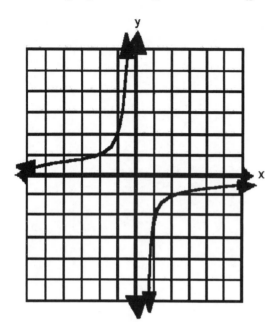

15. Which of the following equations is an example of inverse variation?

    a. $2x = 3y$ b. $\dfrac{x}{y} = \dfrac{7}{5}$ c. $xy = -12$ d. $x + 2y = 4$

16. Which of the following is an example of inverse variation?

    a. $12 = \dfrac{7}{x}$ b. $y = \dfrac{7}{x}$ c. $\dfrac{x}{y} = \dfrac{7}{8}$ d. $\dfrac{x}{3} = \dfrac{y}{8}$

17. If y varies inversely as x and y is 9 when x is 4, find y when x is 12.

    a. 27 b. 17 c. 3 d. 1

18. If y varies inversely as x and y is -12 when x is 6, find y when x is -8.

    a. 9 b. -9 c. 16 d. -16

19. If y varies inversely as x and y is $\dfrac{1}{2}$ when x is 60, find x when y is $\dfrac{3}{4}$.

    a. 45 b. 40 c. 90 d. 32

20. The frequency of a radio wave varies inversely as its wavelength. If a 300-meter wave has a frequency of 400 kilocycles, what is the wavelength of a wave with a frequency of 200 kilocycles?

    a. 150 meters b. 250 meters c. 500 meters d. 600 meters

21. The speeds of the gears on a bicycle are inversely proportional to the number of teeth. If a gear with 20 teeth revolves at a speed of 400 revolutions per minute, at what speed should a gear with 40 teeth revolve?

    a. 800 revolutions per minute b. 500 revolutions per minute
    c. 200 revolutions per minute d. 100 revolutions per minute

22. Simplify: $\dfrac{4x + 12}{4}$.

    a. $x + 3$ b. $x + 12$ c. $x + 8$ d. $4x + 3$

23. Simplify: $\dfrac{15 + 10x}{5}$.

    a. $3 + 10x$ b. $10 + 5x$ c. $3 + 2x$ d. $15 + 2x$

24. Simplify: $\dfrac{6x + 9}{3x}$.

    a. $2 + 3x$ b. $\dfrac{2x + 3}{x}$ c. $\dfrac{2x + 9}{x}$ d. $\dfrac{2 + 3x}{3}$

25. Simplify: $\dfrac{5x - 20}{x - 4}$.

    a. $4x - 5$ b. $4x + 5$ c. $5x - 16$ d. 5

26. Simplify: $\dfrac{8x + 4}{2x + 1}$.

    a. 8 b. $6x + 3$ c. 4 d. $4x + 4$

27. Simplify: $\dfrac{2x + 6}{x^2 - 9}$.

    a. $\dfrac{5}{x - 3}$ b. $\dfrac{2}{x - 3}$ c. $\dfrac{2x + 2}{x^2 - 3}$ d. $\dfrac{2x}{x^2 - 3}$

28. Simplify: $\dfrac{x^2 + 2x - 8}{x^2 - 2x - 24}$.

    a. $-x + 3$ b. $x + 3$ c. $\dfrac{x - 2}{x - 6}$ d. $\dfrac{x - 1}{x - 3}$

29. Simplify: $\dfrac{5}{2x} \cdot \dfrac{4x^2}{5}$.

    a. $10x^3$ b. $10x$ c. $2x^3$ d. $2x$

30. Simplify: $\dfrac{x(x + 3)}{x - 4} \cdot \dfrac{x - 4}{x^3}$.

    a. $\dfrac{x + 3}{x}$ b. $\dfrac{x + 3}{x^2}$ c. $x^2(x + 3)$ d. $x^4(x + 3)$

31. Simplify: $\dfrac{x^2 - 25}{x^6} \cdot \dfrac{x^3}{x - 5}$.

    a. $\dfrac{5}{x}$ b. $\dfrac{x - 5}{x^2}$ c. $\dfrac{x + 5}{x^3}$ d. $\dfrac{x^5 - 25}{x^7 - 5}$

32. Simplify: $\dfrac{2}{5x} + \dfrac{7}{5x}$.

    a. $\dfrac{9}{5x}$ b. $\dfrac{9}{10x}$ c. $\dfrac{9}{5x^2}$ d. $\dfrac{14}{25x^2}$

33. Simplify: $\dfrac{2}{x} + \dfrac{3}{y}$.

    a. $\dfrac{5}{x + y}$ b. $\dfrac{6}{xy}$ c. $\dfrac{2y + 3x}{x + y}$ d. $\dfrac{2y + 3x}{xy}$

34. Simplify: $\dfrac{3}{x} + \dfrac{2}{x + 1}$.

    a. $\dfrac{5}{2x + 1}$ b. $\dfrac{5x}{x(x + 1)}$ c. $\dfrac{5x + 3}{x(x + 1)}$ d. $\dfrac{6}{x + 1}$

35. Simplify: $\dfrac{2}{x+1}+\dfrac{3}{x+2}$.

   a. $\dfrac{6}{x+2}$ b. $\dfrac{5x+7}{(x+1)(x+2)}$ c. $\dfrac{5}{2x+3}$ d. $\dfrac{5x}{(x+1)(x+2)}$

36. Solve for x: $\dfrac{8}{5x}+\dfrac{16}{25}=\dfrac{8}{x}$.

   a. $x=5$ b. $x=10$ c. $x=6$ d. $x=4$

37. Solve for x: $\dfrac{5}{2x}+\dfrac{2}{3x}=\dfrac{19}{24}$.

   a. $x=10$ b. $x=8$ c. $x=6$ d. $x=4$

38. Solve for x: $\dfrac{x}{x-2}+4=\dfrac{12}{x-2}$.

   a. $x=8$ b. $x=6.5$ c. $x=4$ d. $x=2.5$

39. Solve for x: $\dfrac{2}{3}+\dfrac{5}{x+2}=\dfrac{31}{3x+6}$.

   a. $x=24$ b. $x=18$ c. $x=12$ d. $x=6$

40. Solve for x: $\dfrac{3}{x+2}+\dfrac{2}{x-1}=\dfrac{7}{x+2}$.

   a. $x=6$ b. $x=32$ c. $x=4$ d. $x=24$

41. It takes Tom 4 hours to mow a field, and it takes Bob 6 hours to mow the same field. How long will it take them if they work together?
   a. 10 hours   b. 5 hours   c. 3.6 hours   d. 2.4 hours

42. It would take Shari 8 hours to paint a room, and it would take Molly 12 hours to paint the same room. How long would it take them if they worked together?
   a. 4 hours   b. 4.8 hours   c. 9.6 hours   d. 10 hours

43. Identify the extremes in this proportion: $\dfrac{5}{a}=\dfrac{b}{8}$.

   a. 5 and b b. 5 and 8   c. a and b d. a and 8

44. If $\dfrac{a}{b}=\dfrac{c}{d}$, which of the following is also true?

   a. $\dfrac{a}{b}=\dfrac{d}{c}$ b. $\dfrac{b}{a}=\dfrac{d}{c}$ c. $\dfrac{b}{a}=\dfrac{c}{d}$ d. $\dfrac{b}{a}=\dfrac{a}{d}$

45. Solve for x: $\dfrac{13}{7}=\dfrac{91}{x}$.

   a. $x=85$ b. $x=49$ c. $x=13$ d. $x=7$

46. Solve for x: $\dfrac{x}{18}=\dfrac{x+3}{24}$.

   a. $x=0.5$ b. $x=6$ c. $x=9$ d. $x=32$

47. Solve for x: $\dfrac{x}{32}=\dfrac{9}{2x}$.

   a. $x=\pm144$ b. $x=\pm72$ c. $x=\pm36$ d. $x=\pm12$

48. The measures of two complementary angles are in the ratio 7:11. Find the measures of the angles. The sum of the measures of complementary angles is 90°.
   a. 20° and 70°   b. 25° and 65°   c. 35° and 55°   d. 70° and 110°

49. In a survey at Holdenfield High School 20 students were asked what their favorite class was. Nine of the students answered that math was their favorite class. If there are 900 students at Holdenfield High School, about how many like their math class most?
   a. 405   b. 375   c. 200   d. 180

50. Identify the hypothesis in this statement: If $x = 6$, then $x - 4 = 6 - 4$.
   a. $x - 4 = 6 - 4$ b. $x - 4 = -2$ c. $x = 6$ d. $x = -2$

51. Identify the converse of this statement: If $x + 3 = 8$, then $x = 5$.
   a. If $x - 3 = -8$, then $x = -5$.   b. If $x = -5$, then $x - 3 = -8$.
   c. If $x = 5$, then $x + 3 = 8$.   d. If $5 = -x$, then $8 = 3 - x$.

52. Which property would justify this statement: If $x + 6 = 10$, then $x + 6 - 6 = 10 - 6$?
   a. Addition Property of Equality   b. Subtraction Property of Equality
   c. Addition Property of Zero   d. Distributive Property

53. Which property would justify this statement: If $3(x + 2) = 5$, then $3x + 6 = 5$?
   a. Addition Property of Equality   b. Subtraction Property of Equality
   c. Addition Property of Zero   d. Distributive Property

54. Which property would justify this statement: If $5(x - 4) = 20$, then
   $\frac{5(x - 4)}{5} = \frac{20}{5}$?
   a. Division Property of Equality b. Subtraction Property of Equality
   c. Addition Property of Zero   d. Distributive Property

55. Which of the following would justify this statement: If $x - 4 + 4 = 20$, then $x + 0 = 20$?
   a. Addition Property of Equality   b. Addition Property of Zero
   c. Definition of opposites   d. Distributive Property

56. Which of the following would justify this statement: If $x + 0 = 8$, then $x = 8$?
   a. Addition Property of Equality   b. Addition Property of Zero
   c. Definition of opposites   d. Distributive Property

SHORT ANSWER. Write the answer in the space provided.

57. Evaluate $\frac{x^2 + 5}{x + 3}$ when $x = 4$.

   _____

58. Evaluate $\frac{x + 1}{x^2 + x - 6}$ when $x = 2$.

   _____

59. For which value(s) of x is $\frac{x - 1}{x + 7}$ undefined?

   _____

60. For which value(s) of x is $\frac{x + 5}{x^2 - 9}$ undefined?

   _____

61. Graph: $f(x) = \dfrac{1}{x} - 3$. For which value of x is this function undefined?

_____

62. Graph: $f(x) = \dfrac{1}{x+1} + 2$. Write the vertical asymptote of this function.

_____

63. Graph: $f(x) = \dfrac{-1}{x-3}$. Write the vertical asymptote of this function.

_____

64. What must be true if y varies inversely as x?

_____

65. If y varies inversely as x and y is 12 when x is 10, find y when x is 8.

_____

66. If y varies inversely as x and y is 3 when x is 30, find x when y is -15.

_____

67. If y varies inversely as x and y is 60 when x is $\dfrac{2}{3}$, find y when x is $\dfrac{2}{5}$.

_____

68. The length of time that a trip takes is inversely proportional to the average speed traveled during the trip. If a train takes 12 hours to make a trip when traveling at an average of 55 miles per hour, how long will it take to make the same trip when the train is traveling at 60 miles per hour? Using t for time and s for speed, write and solve an equation to represent this problem.

_____

69. The number of vibrations of a guitar string varies inversely as the length of the string. If a string that is 35 cm long vibrates 450 times per second, how long is a string that vibrates 630 times per second? Using n for the number of vibrations and l for length, write and solve an equation to represent this problem.

_____

70. The frequency of a radio wave varies inversely as its wavelength. If a 500-meter wave has a frequency of 4000 kilocycles, what is the frequency of an 800-meter wave? Using f for frequency and l for wavelength, write and solve an equation to represent this problem.

_____

71. Simplify: $\dfrac{15x - 21}{3}$.

_____

72. Simplify: $\dfrac{10 + 8x}{6x}$.

_____

73. Simplify: $\dfrac{8(x + 2)(x + 1)}{24(x + 1)}$.

_____

74. Simplify: $\dfrac{12(x - 6)}{6(x - 3)}$.

_____

75. Simplify: $\dfrac{x - 4}{x^2 - 16}$.

_____

76. Simplify: $\dfrac{x^2 + 5x + 6}{x^2 + 7x + 12}$.

_____

77. Simplify: $\dfrac{x^2 - 25}{x^2 - 3x - 10}$.

_____

78. Simplify: $\dfrac{5x^6}{2} \cdot \dfrac{6}{x^2}$.

_____

79. Simplify: $\dfrac{x + 1}{x} \cdot \dfrac{x + 4}{4}$.

_____

80. Simplify: $\dfrac{x^2 - 9}{4} \cdot \dfrac{12}{x^2 + 6x + 9}$.

_____

81. Simplify: $\dfrac{3}{7x} + \dfrac{5}{7x}$.

_____

82. Simplify: $\dfrac{3}{x} + \dfrac{7}{x - 2}$.

_____

83. Simplify: $\dfrac{2}{x + 2} + \dfrac{4}{x + 5}$.

_____

84. Simplify: $\dfrac{2}{x-3} + \dfrac{7}{x^2 + 2x - 15}$.

_____

85. Solve for x: $\dfrac{3}{x} + \dfrac{3}{4} = \dfrac{36}{4x}$.

_____

86. Solve for x: $\dfrac{x}{x-3} + 5 = \dfrac{21}{x-3}$.

_____

87. Solve for x: $\dfrac{2}{7} + \dfrac{3}{x+3} = \dfrac{45}{7x+21}$.

_____

88. Solve for x: $\dfrac{1}{4} + \dfrac{3}{x+3} = \dfrac{23}{4x+12}$.

_____

89. Solve for x: $\dfrac{2}{x+3} + \dfrac{3}{x-1} = \dfrac{4}{x-1}$.

_____

90. It would take Chris 9 hours to load a truck, and it would take Jesse 11 hours to load the same truck. Write and solve an equation to find how long it would take them to load the truck if they worked together.

_____

91. It would take Chad 10 hours to plow a field. It would take Sam 15 hours to plow the same field. Write and solve an equation to find how long would it take to plow the field if they worked together.

_____

92. Identify the means and extremes of this proportion: $\dfrac{3}{y} = \dfrac{x}{4}$.

_____

93. If $\dfrac{a}{b} = \dfrac{c}{d}$, is $\dfrac{a}{c} = \dfrac{b}{d}$ also true? Explain.

_____

94. Solve for x: $\dfrac{23}{x} = \dfrac{345}{195}$.

_____

95. Solve for x: $\dfrac{x+6}{21} = \dfrac{x}{12}$.

_____

96. Solve for x: $\dfrac{5x}{16} = \dfrac{20}{x}$.

_____

97. A recipe for stew that feeds 20 people calls for 6 pounds of beef. How many pounds of beef are needed to make this recipe for 50 people? Write and solve a proportion to represent this problem.

_____

98. It costs \$345 to carpet 24 ft^2 of floor. How much will it cost to cover 60 ft^2 of floor with the same carpet? Write and solve a proportion to represent this problem.

_____

99. Identify the hypothesis and the conclusion in this statement: If $x = 2$, then $x + 8 = 2 + 8$.

_____

100. Write the converse of this statement: If $x = -2$, then $x^2 = 4$. Is the converse true?

_____

101. Write the converse of this statement: If $x - 6 = 4$, then $x = 10$. Is the converse true?

_____

102. Prove: If $x + 8 = 12$, then $x = 4$. Give a reason for each step.

103. Prove: If $\dfrac{2}{3}x = 10$, then $x = 15$. Give a reason for each step.

104. Prove: If $\dfrac{3}{4}x - 5 = 4$, then $x = 12$. Give a reason for each step.

105. Prove: If $\dfrac{2}{3}x + 6 = 10$, then $x = 6$. Give a reason for each step.

ANSWERS TO CHAPTER 10

1. Answer: a Section: 1 Objective: 1a

2. Answer: a Section: 2 Objective: 2b

3. Answer: c Section: 3 Objective: 3a

4. Answer: a Section: 4 Objective: 4a

5. Answer: b Section: 5 Objective: 5a

6. Answer: b Section: 6 Objective: 6c

7. Answer: c Section: 7 Objective: 7b

8. Answer: c. 2 Section: 1 Objective: 1a

9. Answer: d. undefined Section: 1 Objective: 1a

10. Answer: b. $x = -3$ Section: 1 Objective: 1b

11. Answer: d. $x = -5$ or $x = 1$ Section: 1 Objective: 1b

12. Answer:
    a. $f(x) = \dfrac{1}{x + 2}$

    Section: 1 Objective: 1c

13. Answer:
    b. $f(x) = \dfrac{1}{x - 2} - 1$

    Section: 1 Objective: 1c

14. Answer:
    c. $f(x) = \dfrac{-2}{x}$

    Section: 1 Objective: 1c

15. Answer: c. $xy = -12$ Section: 2 Objective: 2a

16. Answer:
    b. $y = \dfrac{7}{x}$

    Section: 2 Objective: 2a

17. Answer: c. 3   Section: 2   Objective: 2b

18. Answer: a. 9   Section: 2   Objective: 2b

19. Answer: b. 40   Section: 2   Objective: 2b

20. Answer: d. 600 meters   Section: 2   Objective: 2b

21. Answer: c. 200 revolutions per minute   Section: 2   Objective: 2b

22. Answer: a. $x + 3$ Section: 3   Objective: 3a

23. Answer: c. $3 + 2x$ Section: 3   Objective: 3a

24. Answer:
b. $\dfrac{2x + 3}{x}$

Section: 3   Objective: 3a

25. Answer: d. 5   Section: 3   Objective: 3a

26. Answer: c. 4   Section: 3   Objective: 3a

27. Answer:
b. $\dfrac{2}{x - 3}$

Section: 3   Objective: 3a

28. Answer:
c. $\dfrac{x - 2}{x - 6}$

Section: 3   Objective: 3a

29. Answer: d. $2x$ Section: 4   Objective: 4a

30. Answer:
b. $\dfrac{x + 3}{x^2}$

Section: 4   Objective: 4a

31. Answer:
c. $\dfrac{x + 5}{x^3}$

Section: 4   Objective: 4a

32. Answer:
a. $\dfrac{9}{5x}$

Section: 4   Objective: 4b

33. Answer:

   d. $\dfrac{2y + 3x}{xy}$

   Section: 4   Objective: 4b

34. Answer:

   c. $\dfrac{5x + 3}{x(x + 1)}$

   Section: 4   Objective: 4b

35. Answer:

   b. $\dfrac{5x + 7}{(x + 1)(x + 2)}$

   Section: 4   Objective: 4b

36. Answer: b. $x = 10$ Section: 5   Objective: 5a

37. Answer: d. $x = 4$ Section: 5   Objective: 5a

38. Answer: c. $x = 4$ Section: 5   Objective: 5a

39. Answer: d. $x = 6$ Section: 5   Objective: 5a

40. Answer: c. $x = 4$ Section: 5   Objective: 5a

41. Answer: d. 2.4 hours   Section: 5   Objective: 5b

42. Answer: b. 4.8 hours   Section: 5   Objective: 5b

43. Answer: b. 5 and 8   Section: 6   Objective: 6a

44. Answer:

   b. $\dfrac{b}{a} = \dfrac{d}{c}$

   Section: 6   Objective: 6b

45. Answer: b. $x = 49$ Section: 6   Objective: 6c

46. Answer: c. $x = 9$ Section: 6   Objective: 6c

47. Answer: d. $x = \pm12$ Section: 6   Objective: 6c

48. Answer: c. 35° and 55°   Section: 6   Objective: 6c

49. Answer: a. 405   Section: 6   Objective: 6c

50. Answer: c. $x = 6$ Section: 7   Objective: 7a

51. Answer: c. If $x = 5$, then $x + 3 = 8$.   Section: 7   Objective: 7a

52. Answer: b. Subtraction Property of Equality   Section: 7   Objective: 7b

53. Answer: d. Distributive Property   Section: 7   Objective: 7b

54. Answer: a. Division Property of Equality   Section: 7   Objective: 7b

55. Answer: c. Definition of opposites   Section: 7   Objective: 7b

56. Answer: b. Addition Property of Zero   Section: 7   Objective: 7b

57. Answer: 3   Section: 1   Objective: 1a

58. Answer: undefined   Section: 1   Objective: 1a

59. Answer: $x = -7$ Section: 1   Objective: 1b

60. Answer: $x = 3$ or $x = -3$ Section: 1   Objective: 1b

61. Answer: $x = 0$

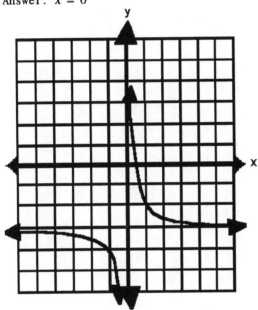

   Section: 1   Objective: 1c

62. Answer: The vertical asymptote is at $x = -1$.

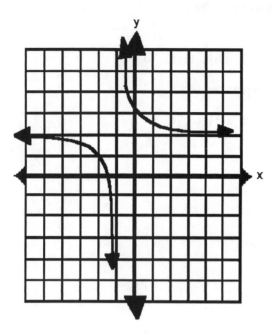

Section: 1 Objective: 1c

63. Answer: The vertical asymptote is at $x = 3$.

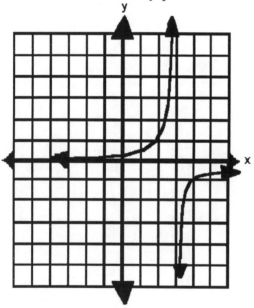

Section: 1 Objective: 1c

64. Answer:

$xy = k$, or $y = \dfrac{k}{x}$, where $x \neq 0$ and k is a constant

Section: 2 Objective: 2a

65. Answer: $y = 15$ Section: 2   Objective: 2b

66. Answer: $x = -6$ Section: 2   Objective: 2b

67. Answer: $y = 100$ Section: 2   Objective: 2b

68. Answer: $ts = k$, so $k = 12 \times 55 = 660$; $60t = 660$; $t = 11$ hours   Section: 2   Objective: 2b

69. Answer: $nl = k$ so $k = 450 \times 35 = 15,750$; $630l = 15,750$; $l = 25$ cm   Section: 2

   Objective: 2b

70. Answer: $fl = k$, so $k = 4000 \times 500 = = 2,000,000$; $800f = 2,000,000$; $f = 2500$ kilocycles

   Section: 2   Objective: 2b

71. Answer: $5x - 7$ Section: 3   Objective: 3a

72. Answer:
   $$\frac{5 + 4x}{3x}$$
   Section: 3   Objective: 3a

73. Answer:
   $$\frac{x + 2}{3}$$
   Section: 3   Objective: 3a

74. Answer:
   $$\frac{2(x - 6)}{x - 3}$$
   Section: 3   Objective: 3a

75. Answer:
   $$\frac{1}{x + 4}$$
   Section: 3   Objective: 3a

76. Answer:
   $$\frac{x + 2}{x + 4}$$
   Section: 3   Objective: 3a

77. Answer:
   $$\frac{x + 5}{x + 2}$$
   Section: 3   Objective: 3a

78. Answer: $15x^4$ Section: 4 Objective: 4a

79. Answer:
$$\frac{(x + 1)(x + 4)}{4x} = \frac{x^2 + 5x + 4}{4x}$$
Section: 4 Objective: 4a

80. Answer:
$$\frac{3(x - 3)}{x + 3} = \frac{3x - 9}{x + 3}$$
Section: 4 Objective: 4a

81. Answer:
$$\frac{8}{7x}$$
Section: 4 Objective: 4b

82. Answer:
$$\frac{10x - 6}{x(x - 2)}$$
Section: 4 Objective: 4b

83. Answer:
$$\frac{6x + 18}{(x + 2)(x + 5)}$$
Section: 4 Objective: 4b

84. Answer:
$$\frac{2x + 17}{(x + 5)(x - 3)} = \frac{2x + 17}{x^2 + 2x - 15}$$
Section: 4 Objective: 4b

85. Answer: $x = 8$ Section: 5 Objective: 5a

86. Answer: $x = 6$ Section: 5 Objective: 5a

87. Answer: $x = 9$ Section: 5 Objective: 5a

88. Answer: $x = 8$ Section: 5 Objective: 5a

89. Answer: $x = 5$ Section: 5 Objective: 5a

90. Answer:
$$\frac{x}{9} + \frac{x}{11} = 1; \ x = 4.95; \ 4.95 \text{ hours}$$
Section: 5 Objective: 5b

91. Answer:

$\frac{x}{10} + \frac{x}{15} = 1$; $x = 6$; 6 hours

Section: 5 Objective: 5b

92. Answer: means: x and y; extremes: 3 and 4 Section: 6 Objective: 6a

93. Answer: yes; $ad = bc$ in both cases Section: 6 Objective: 6b

94. Answer: $x = 13$ Section: 6 Objective: 6c

95. Answer: $x = 8$ Section: 6 Objective: 6c

96. Answer: $x = \pm 8$ Section: 6 Objective: 6c

97. Answer:

$\frac{6}{20} = \frac{x}{50}$, $x = 15$; 15 pounds of beef

Section: 6 Objective: 6c

98. Answer:

$\frac{345}{24} = \frac{x}{60}$, $x = 862.5$; \$862.50

Section: 6 Objective: 6c

99. Answer: hypothesis: $x = 2$; conclusion: $x + 8 = 2 + 8$ Section: 7 Objective: 7a

100. Answer: If $x^2 = 4$, then $x = -2$; no, if $x^2 = 4$, then $x = \pm 2$. Section: 7 Objective: 7a

101. Answer: If $x = 10$, then $x - 6 = 4$; yes. Section: 7 Objective: 7a

102. Answer:

$x + 8 = 12$	Hypothesis or given
$x + 8 - 8 = 12 - 8$	Subtraction Property of Equality
$x + 0 = 4$	Definition of opposites; simplify
$x = 0$	Addition Property of Zero

Section: 7 Objective: 7b

103. Answer:

$\frac{2}{3}x = 10$	Hypothesis or given
$\frac{3}{2} \cdot \frac{2}{3}x = \frac{3}{2} \cdot 10$	Multiplication Property of Equality
$1 \cdot x = 15$	Definition of reciprocals; simplify
$x = 15$	Multiplication Property of One

Section: 7 Objective: 7b

104. Answer:

$$\frac{3}{4}x - 5 = 4$$ Hypothesis or given

$$\frac{3}{4}x - 5 + 5 = 4 + 5$$ Addition Property of Equality

$$\frac{3}{4}x + 0 = 9$$ Definition of opposites; simplify

$$\frac{3}{4}x = 9$$ Addition Property of Zero

$$\frac{4}{3} \cdot \frac{3}{4}x = \frac{4}{3} \cdot 9$$ Multiplication Property of Equality

$1 \cdot x = 12$ Definition of reciprocals; simplify

$x = 12$ Multiplication Property of One

Section: 7   Objective: 7b

105. Answer:

$$\frac{2}{3}x + 6 = 10$$ Hypothesis or given

$$\frac{2}{3}x + 6 - 6 = 10 - 6$$ Subtraction Property of Equality

$$\frac{2}{3}x + 0 = 4$$ Definition of opposites; simplify

$$\frac{2}{3}x = 4$$ Addition Property of Zero

$$\frac{3}{2} \cdot \frac{2}{3}x = \frac{3}{2} \cdot 4$$ Multiplication Property of Equality

$1 \cdot x = 6$ Definition of reciprocals; simplify

$x = 6$ Multiplication Property of One

Section: 7   Objective: 7b